Connecting Two Worlds

An Environmental Journey from Peace Corps to Present

Connecting Two Worlds

An Environmental Journey from Peace Corps to Present

Anthony Simeone

A Peace Corps Writers Book

Connecting Two Worlds
An Environmental Journey
From Peace Corps To Present

An imprint of Peace Corps Worldwide

Copyright © 2013 by Anthony Simeone
All rights reserved.

Printed in the United States of America
by Peace Corps Writers of Oakland, California.

No part of this book may be used or reproduced in any manner whatsoever without written permission except in the case of brief quotations contained in critical articles or reviews.

For more information, contact
peacecorpsworldwide@gmail.com.
Peace Corps Writers and the Peace Corps Writers colophon are trademarks of
PeaceCorpsWorldwide.org.

ISBN: 1-935-92512-1
ISBN: 978-1-935-92512-5
Library of Congress Control Number: 2013933071

First Peace Corps Writers Edition, February 2013

Dedication

To Margaret for her support in making our journey meaningful.

To Claire and Tom for their willingness to take the next steps of their personal journeys.

To all of the volunteer and humanitarian organizations that have supported and continue to support the growing need for improving the lives of so many people throughout the developing world.

Acknowledgments

My experiences in the Peace Corps were enhanced by my relationship with Ambassador Richard Matheron and his wife Kay. They have continued to remain close friends, a constant reminder of and connection to those early years. It was the Ambassador who provided an important link that would become the genesis of my company and inspiration to write this book. In spite of her numerous diplomatic responsibilities, Kay understood the importance of providing some wonderful chocolate chip cookies to bring back a taste of home. Today, she has provided important editorial comments and suggestions to help move this work to completion.

Most importantly, this book would not have been possible without the complete support and encouragement of my wife, Margaret. Her ability to artfully engage in the creation and editing processes has been invaluable in creating my belief that I could actually write this book.

Connecting Two Worlds

An Environmental Journey from Peace Corps to Present

Contents

	Prologue vii
A yembre	1. Sustainability 1
A yiibu	2. Civilization 7
A taabo	3. Worlds Apart 12
A naase	4. Ouagadougou... 18
A nu	5. Travel 32
A yoobe	6. Animism/Charlatan/Injury 45
A yopoe	7. Food/Nutrition/Drink 58
A nii	8. Knowledge of the Universe................. 71
A wɛ	9. Life in a Village 80
A piiga	10. The Well 106
A pig la a ye	11. Closure... 114
	Epilogue 122
	Glossary.. 125

The words used in the Contents and Chapter headings are taken from Mòoré, the language of the Mossi and national language of Burkina Faso.

Prologue

> "You make a living by what you get. You make a life by what you give."
>
> Winston Churchill

Connecting Two Worlds is a metaphor for the contrasting elements in this book. The two planetary images on the cover were chosen to establish the backdrop for this stark contrast. The visual differences between Planet Earth and Mars are obvious. The Blue Planet represents a fertile, living environment. The Red Planet is stark and dead. Earth has an abundance of water and a balance of atmospheric gasses conducive to human life. Mars has *potential* underground reserves and an atmosphere that is comprised almost entirely of carbon dioxide – toxic to human life.

Two Worlds is also a contrast between my life and experiences as a Peace Corps Volunteer in West Africa and my life in the more environmentally friendly Mid-Atlantic States on the east coast of the United States.

Even more deeply, *Two Worlds* is a book about connecting the dots between the influence of population and the growing degradation of Earth's environment. Becoming the most dominant species on Earth has come at a huge cost. Our success in becoming more globalized has caused a major disruption to local cultures/traditions as well as to the environment. For a very long time, this was believed to be the pathway to progress.

Years ago, my world history professor in college shared an insightful observation. History, he said, is a spiral. Throughout history, the same or similar events continue to present themselves as if new to the world.

Humans continue to make the same mistakes, offering the same but updated list of excuses and justifications supporting their resistance to change. You can be sure that the events and excuses that have occurred in our distant past will return again far in the future. It is only the participating players who will change.

The Blue Planet is losing portions of its protective ozone layer because of human negligence in managing the health of our global ecosystems. Is it possible for humans to push the environmental balance beyond recovery so that in time, Earth and Mars will become more visibly and environmentally similar?

A yembre

1

Sustainability

"The recognition that things that are not sustainable will eventually come to an end does not give us much of a guide to whether the transition will be calm or exciting."

Timothy Geithner

This year marks the 50th Anniversary of the founding of the Peace Corps, a milestone that on its own merits could have given me reason to write this book. However, the association was purely coincidental. What really prompted me was my desire to focus attention on the myriad environmental issues confronting our planet today – the very same issues that challenged my corner of a drought-stricken region in West Africa as a Peace Corps Volunteer.

The stories I offer are examples of larger scale global issues that now threaten each and every one of us, far beyond the conditions that have persisted throughout this western

African region in the Sahel. While these stories may seem foreign to our current lifestyles, they have far reaching implications for our future lives and what may become our new normal.

These global conditions are accelerating at an unprecedented pace. To better understand their potential impact, it may be useful to look to the past. It has only been 12,000 years since the introduction of agriculture. This was an important first step in human societal development that enabled the growth of towns and cities by providing consistent, and reproducible sources of nutrition. However, for that step in evolution to occur, one more ingredient was necessary: stable and reasonably predictable climate.

Without climate stability, there would have been little success in agriculture because of the delicate environmental tolerances needed for plants to survive and reproduce. With climate stability, the world would eventually explode with human activity. This explosion has been the most dramatic in the 20th and 21st centuries.

Today, every part of our planet is accessible – and therein lies the problem. A shift in our way of thinking is required to meet the growing demands for food. Productive agriculture can no longer take a backseat to the ever-growing consumer demand for manufactured goods.

To meet these growing agricultural needs, an important scientific milestone was achieved in Mexico in the 1940s when scientists began to understand the granular details of DNA mapping that enabled the development of new, scientifically engineered varieties of disease resistant, high-yield wheat. Advances continued for the next twenty years and culminated with the rise of what is now known as the Green Revolution.

The science behind this advancement was important. While science has continued to pursue advances in genetic modification (GMO), this success is also creating a global fear that we may be sacrificing nature's proven, evolutionary process for an unproven short-term remedy. What if science is wrong about the formula to reengineer nature?

Perhaps the most important ingredient for science and nature to be successful was the availability of ample supplies of water to irrigate this new era in agriculture. It is the timing required for the occurrences of moisture and heat that varies from crop to crop. If this timing is disrupted for extended periods, longer-term consequences are inevitable. We have recently witnessed the damage caused to crops from excessive heat and inadequate rainfall in the farm-belt of the United States. Recovery will be costly. Each successive recurrence will be even more costly.

Circumstances were much different in the past. To take advantage of extensive waterway networks, rivers were dammed or diverted. Today, few major rivers remain that have not been harnessed by dams. There have been lessons learned to provide a better understanding of the pros and cons of dams that has led to dam removals to restore a river's natural flow.

If rivers were not easily accessible, regions could rely on the water from underground aquifers. The availability of fresh water seemed limitless. Those clean reserves of underground water from previously untapped aquifers are being depleted at the expense of future availability. Changing climate is having an impact on global weather patterns. The resulting change in the distribution of rainfall is causing new problems for many of the world's most productive farmlands.

My first encounter with these extreme environmental conditions was in French West Africa. Sub-Saharan Africa has not been blessed with vast mineral reserves or sweeping savannahs for large herds of predator and prey to roam. Devastated by years of famine, drought and degraded lifestyles, its growing population is even more challenged by the poor quality of its degraded land. Yet, in spite of these deficiencies, large, multinational companies continue to search for the next mineral lode to be used in future production.

A world that has been accelerating a philosophy of global availability of goods and services may be rapidly forced to accept a new paradigm: the realization that our planet is unable to sustain the consumption demands that result from uncontrolled population growth.

The majority of earth's growing population has occurred since the early 19th Century when the planet had just one billion people. By the 1920s – just one hundred twenty-five years later – population had doubled to two billion. By 1960, the global population was three billion people. Today, the global population hovers at seven billion and is expected to reach nine billion by 2050! The successful resolution of managing the demands of more people with the need to consume less remains unclear.

The planet is entering a new and uncharted phase of environmental health – unlike anything experienced by our ancestors. The delicate balance between our ability to favorably reverse current environmental trends or staying our present course is uncertain. At stake is no longer just the fate of the world's most destitute – the bottom billion, but of those countries teetering on political instability and social unrest. These are the countries with little production capacity and growing populations of under-trained women and unemployed/undereducated youth. These will be the countries most likely to replicate future occurrences of Arab Spring.

As climate change becomes more frequent and more dramatic in scale, the environmental impact will only exacerbate the political instability of these endangered countries. The memories of what I saw as a Volunteer so many years ago have become a second reality for what the world is experiencing today and the stakes are much higher.

The Industrialized countries have contributed most to our planet's environmental degradation and they must be proactive in the creation of acceptable and executable corrective solutions.

The foundation for writing this book comes from my experiences as a Volunteer when the seeds of these experiences were first planted. Today, those seeds have germinated into my vision: (1) to share details of the world's growing environmental challenges and of understanding their relevancy in today's world; and (2) to illustrate the impact that earth's ever expanding population is having on the sustainability of our planet.

For greater detail of the environmental terms found in the Glossary, please visit the "Issues" section of my website: http://dimidia.com/issues/.

A yiibu
2

Civilization

"The greatest threat to our planet is the belief that someone else will save it."

Robert Swan
1st person to walk to both Poles

Each Volunteer's experiences are unique. No single volume, regardless of size, can provide representative examples of lifestyles for all of the 200,000+ Volunteers in the more than 138 countries the Peace Corps has served since its founding in 1961. However, I feel confident that the experiences shared by all Volunteers would resemble in style and substance those offered here.

There is a lot of maturity and personal growth that comes from participating as a Volunteer in a Peace Corps immersion program. It was not until I returned home that I realized that my numerous photographs and correspondence may have helped family and friends to participate in those experiences but could never reproduce the sensations derived from personal immersion into a strange and new cultural arena.

My term of service in the Peace Corps well-digging program was from 1971 to 1973 in a small village named Dablo in the northern region of Upper Volta (now Burkina Faso). There had been a Volunteer living and working in my region for three years prior to my arrival. In a way, you could say that my term was pre-conditioned by the experiences they shared with him.

By the end of his third year, his immersion into the region was so effective, that he acquired the Islamic name of Moussa. After two years, I remained, as I came in, Mr. Tony. I quickly learned that his success posed both benefits and problems for me as a Volunteer. My arrival was neither shocking nor traumatic – at least not shocking for most of the villages I would be working in. I was able to tell immediately when someone was absolutely shocked, intrigued or ambivalent by my presence.

There was one woman whose erratic behavior became quite pronounced as I arrived in her village for the very first time. As I emerged from our supply truck, I began approaching the mixed group of men and women, young and old. As I walked closer, one woman began to back away from me. I intentionally took a few more steps towards her and she receded the same number of steps away from me. I decided to make this a game and began to walk around the truck.

Everyone but the woman understood this had become a game. When I finally stopped and asked why she was afraid of me, she answered very simply that she had never before seen a white person. Even though she heard me speak, touched my skin and felt my hair, she could not equate me with herself or her family or neighbors. I could not be explained and that made her fearful.

I hope you will be able to appreciate the context in which these experiences occurred as well as the sensations that I, and every other Volunteer who has served in one of the recipient countries, may have derived from their occurrence.

Today, the game has changed. Not so much for those still challenged by a life in sub-Saharan Africa. Their lives remain as challenging as ever. The environment I experienced in West Africa is now appearing with greater frequency around the world and is beginning to impact more people in more locations. Climate change could soon force the Maldive Islands in the Pacific to be swallowed by rising ocean levels while the increased frequency and severity of seasonal storms are likely to become the rule and no longer the exception for many parts of the world.

These changes are having an even more dramatic impact on animal reproduction cycles, plant growth cycles and species survival. It becomes dangerous for trees and plants should temperatures begin to prematurely rise and become warmer. Just small changes will encourage plants to bud and bloom earlier than usual rather than with the predictable safety of their normal seasonal cycles that have evolved over millions of years. Bird migration cycles will be disrupted as will the availability of their insect-related nutritional needs.

Survival of the Arctic Snowshoe Hare is just one of many examples that shows how abnormal changes in the onset of a season can have a dramatic impact on the survival of a species. One of the hare's most important survival techniques is the change in the color of its fur from brown to snow white with the coincident arrival of seasonal snowfall. If the onset of seasonal snow is delayed too long, the hare will turn white long before the arrival of nature's first snowfalls and contrast sharply with the still remaining brown, fall colors. The hare, of course, will be unaware of this color imbalance. This false security will make it an easy target for its primary predator – the lynx. Eventually, the natural balance will have been disrupted long enough to enable the lynx to decimate the hare population – forcing it into extinction.

Yes, the game is changing and species will be more challenged than ever to rapidly adapt to these changes or disappear. What remains very clear is that species adaptation cannot be forced. It must evolve. It is simply unable to occur at such a rapid pace as our planet's environmental changes are occurring today.

There is little question that since the Industrial Revolution, Homo Sapiens has become the dominant species on our planet. This dominance has come at a cost. Our "success" has contributed to an unprecedented growth in population, climate change and loss of bio-diversity. In our efforts to improve our overall quality of life, science has exploited nature with the development of innumerable drugs. Science has used petroleum products to create even newer and more powerful "petro"chemicals that are now being indiscriminately flushed into our oceans, rivers, groundwater and atmosphere. Our success to continue as a species depends on the health and productive capacities of the world's biodiversity and ecosystem services. Like the lynx and snow hare, when these polarities become too out-of-balance, they can no longer continue to safely coexist.

A taabo
3

Worlds Apart

"Look! Look! Look deep into nature and you will understand everything."

Albert Einstein

How Deep?

One of the police came to my door and asked if he could speak to me in private. We were friends so, although unusual, I did not consider this would be anything but a social call – serious, but social. He asked if he could close the door because he wanted to discuss some safety concerns about a well that his friends were digging.

At this point, I was really hoping I hadn't suggested to him that I actually knew more than I did about the well-digging process.

We sat at a table and he began to share his concern. His friend was digging a very deep well. One of my deepest wells was just over one hundred feet deep. The well his friends had dug so far was nearly two hundred twenty-five feet deep. I agreed that it was a very deep well. One concern in digging a large diameter well is the structural integrity of the wall. I was preparing to discuss my concerns about wall integrity.

He leaned across the table, looked directly at my eyes and, speaking even more slowly, asked again: "How deep can he dig the well?" I guess he thought that by leaning forward, looking directly at me and speaking slowly he would make me understand his concern even better. Remember, this conversation is taking place in a remote village, deep in the bush of West Africa during a severe drought. Water tables were falling and wells were going dry. Not being a hydrological engineer, I wasn't confident I knew the answer.

What he REALLY wanted to know was how deep his friend could dig a well down into the earth before falling through to the other side of the planet! He waited for my answer.

For me, this story focuses on a stark reality in the developing world; one in which a very limited knowledge of the outside world, while living daily with life and death struggles, negates much of the need for "real-world science facts". In his world, it was still possible to fall through the Earth!

These stories represent not only my experiences as a Peace Corps volunteer in Western Africa, but also my passionate interest in helping adults understand that the way we treat our global environment today is shaping our futures and ultimately our interdependence on one another around the world. One of those people might just be another naïve policeman looking for answers to troubling questions or it could be a young child first learning about nature and the environment.

You may think it important to focus on the limited perspective of this policeman who was concerned that his friend might fall out the other end of a very deep well. Yet there are different aspects from the obvious, of this story and the others that follow. You may not initially appreciate or notice that there are not simply cultural differences but environmental similarities to conditions occurring more and more frequently around our world today. We have begun to experience extreme weather events, longer and more frequent periods of drought, and an increased need for humanitarian aid for millions of displaced persons.

Taking this story at face value will not enable you to fully understand the complex process of digging a traditional well. To hand dig a well one hundred feet deep while using just traditional tools and methods is incredibly difficult. The challenge is to dig a well with the smallest possible diameter – just large enough to give the worker freedom of movement and for the worker to be lowered down into the well. The process is very methodical but can also be very slow because of the space restrictions. The loosened soil will fill a calabash with dirt that will then be hoisted to the surface.

This process is repeated for several hours at a time and could easily extend down for thirty to fifty feet deep. When the day's dig is stopped, the worker will be carefully hoisted to the surface. The "rider", seated on a two feet wide wooden seat made from the thick branch of a scrub bush or small tree, is always at the mercy of the men controlling the rope. In order to do this work, any anxiety or claustrophobia must be left at ground level.

This story also begs the question of why so much time and energy would go into digging a well so deep. Surely, there are areas where groundwater is more easily accessible than needing to dig a well one hundred fifty feet deep. Has the water table throughout the region fallen because of the continued droughts that have persisted throughout the previous century? Or could the water tables have fallen because the droughts have made the heavily in demand groundwater a more valuable and eagerly sought commodity as most other surface water sources become depleted?

The most important aspect of this story, however, is really about how environmental demands in other areas around the world are beginning to resemble those in this one, small part of a remote region in Africa. How could the environmental causes contributing to finding water in a deep water well being dug in Africa resemble the impact of falling water tables now being experienced throughout the American Southwest or melting glaciers across the high mountain ranges spanning the continents? Have any lessons been learned from the recent twelve yearlong drought in Australia that could apply to the drying patterns being experienced across Texas, Oklahoma, India and China?

Growing populations are placing more stress on already degraded land and water resources around much of the world. Our lifestyles contribute directly to these phenomena. Many scientists still contend these changes *"may be cyclical and we may simply be going into a warmer phase of this cycle."* Just as the policeman was clueless to the knowledge and meaning of Earth's diameter of twenty-five thousand miles, the poorest, bottom two billion people on our planet do not have a clue as to the cyclical nature of ice ages and warm periods.

They do not sit around evening fires after dinner to discuss the anthropogenic causes of a changing climate! They know only that there is less wood available for cooking fires and for building rounded frame huts. They are reminded daily that their wells have too little water for consumption and that crops are failing during seasons that are becoming both too hot and too dry to sustain even meager agricultural productivity.

In developing countries where many of the economies are agriculture-based, the long-term forecast for self-sustainability is bleak. By all forecasts, food subsidies from donor countries will need to increase to offset the population changes throughout the developing world – especially those impacted by climate change.

Brazil, Russia, India, China, South Africa (BRICS) – a powerful group of large emerging economies are taking action to become leaders in implementing sustainable solutions. Because of their population issues these countries understand that sustainability really does matter for the continuous and successful growth of their economies. Sustainability is even more critical for the welfare of their citizens.

The United States has begun to experience greater variability in its national climate and must now begin to accept the reality that environment does matter – whether nationally or internationally. Atmospheric circulation will ensure that one country's environmental behavior will likely influence other countries' weather and air quality around the globe. The time has come to be even more proactive in the engineering and implementation of sustainable solutions.

If you see these threads woven throughout the stories selected, then you will begin to understand the benefits I have derived from being a Peace Corps Volunteer. You may also understand why those past experiences have been the drivers for my interest in raising awareness of environmental issues.

It has become even more critical today for all countries to accept that perhaps in no other period of our planet Earth has our understanding of these tightly-coupled environmental elements been so important. Understanding alone is no longer satisfactory. Appropriate action must be taken to make Earth a more sustainable place to live.

A naase
4

Ouagadougou

"People 'over-produce' pollution because they are not paying for the costs of dealing with it."

Ha-Joon Chang
23 Things They Don't Tell You About Capitalism

Yes, there most definitely is a city by the name of Ouagadougou. Its name means "where people get honor and respect." It is the capital of Burkina Faso, a former French colony in sub-Saharan French West Africa. During my two years in the Peace Corps, the country was the third poorest country in the world. Not much has changed today except the country's rising population from five million in 1971 to a current level of sixteen million in only forty years. Ouagadougou remains its largest city with a population of almost one and a half million.

The city of Ouaga is located in the geographic center of the country. I spent most of my time 185 miles further north in the dryer region of the country known as the Sahel. The Sahel is a 4,500 mile-wide transitional zone that reaches from Senegal in the West to the Sudan in the East – forming the entire southern boundary of the Sahara Desert.

When I first arrived in Ouaga, every sensory experience seemed magnified. The epicenter of this hectic capital was its Grand Marche (Central Market). There, legions of merchants would arrive from distant villages bringing goods to be sold. Until the market burned down in 2003, it was one of the largest markets in West Africa.

One very important engine of commerce that is replicated beyond the Central Market and in each of the smaller town and village markets throughout Africa is price negotiation. Nothing is ever intended to be sold at the asking price.

Learning the basics of this unnatural process came from observation and advice from seasoned volunteers and in-country hosts. Be prepared for a series of exchanges that could last as long as sixty minutes or as little as a few.

Each month, several of us would share a truck and travel to Ouaga for supplies. During our stay, we would always schedule several mandatory visits to the French boulangerie (bakery) often gorging on freshly made éclairs and Napoleons – and too many other cream-filled samplings. Recovery usually took about one day.

Eventually, the urge for these flavorful treats would be satisfied and I could begin the task of spending time with other Volunteers and staff of the Peace Corps and the American Embassy. It did not take long to realize that with such a small, in-country American community, it was possible to derive needed benefits from building quality relationships with Foreign Service staff. These would often include invitations to staff homes for dinners in home-like conditions or unlimited access to the Embassy swimming pool. In return, we needed only to bring our vivid minds and vibrant personalities. On the surface that appeared to be a fair exchange. In reality, the advantage was clearly in favor of the recipient Volunteer.

The Peace Corps Hostel was an important social center for Volunteers. It was not a conspicuous building but the availability of running water, electricity and a full kitchen made it feel like a retreat…even with herds of cattle, sheep, or goats often walking down the street in front of the entrance gate.

Occasionally, an interesting visitor would pass through. An overnight was often all that was needed. It came with shower and breakfast. But the heart of the visitors coming to Ouaga was the 60+ Volunteers who worked throughout the country. We clearly understood that our cultural benefits and obligations remained in our villages and not from long stays in the capital. We enjoyed getting rejuvenated with showers, meals – that varied greatly from our daily meals in our villages, and some good conversations, in English, of course. With too much time spent in our villages, English could easily become a second language.

Environment

Ouagadougou, like many urban centers in sub-Saharan Africa and throughout the developing world has been experiencing an increased flow of people from rural villages. Factors contributing to this movement are the diminishing return of meaningful employment and educational opportunities for youth, deteriorating land quality contributing to noticeable reductions in agricultural productivity and population. As the relationship between land and people moves from one of equilibrium to decline, the potential to recover once productive farmland becomes more challenging. This human-induced (anthropogenic) deterioration of land quality is known as desertification.

This movement of people also suggests that when conditions in rural areas worsen, cities provide migrants with a false and uncertain opportunity to begin a better life. They believe that if they are able to secure job opportunities in professions other than agriculture, they will improve their standard of living. In fact, the opportunities will be fewer and of a lower quality because factors – such as education – will prevent these migrants from being assimilated into the fabric of the cities to secure anything other than a low wage service position or unemployment. The net result is a growing proportion of welfare recipients.

For as bad as this may seem, a more insidious impact of migration is the abandonment and permanent loss of established village traditions and practices that have evolved over millennia – practices which enabled survival in these hostile, rural areas. It could be the spiritual rites of the traditional healer or the medicinal value of specialized herbs and plants. Once lost to urban life, this knowledge is gone forever.

The impact of this increasing number of urban migrants is the "over" growth of cities into mega-cities. Studies on urban growth present two clearly opposing viewpoints.

The optimistic view is that a rapidly growing mega-city can, in itself, become more like a city-state where the benefits of urban versus rural living combine with the relative ease of delivering basic services. These qualities can raise the living standards for billions of future rural migrants integrated into a fully functional urban society.

The pessimistic view suggests that the arrival of huge numbers of rural migrants will only increase stress in the recipient urban centers. Unable to meet the growing social service demands of these growing numbers, cities will begin to struggle with the allocation of scarce resources. The incidence of disease will rise and violence will increase.

The stress from population movement is occurring far beyond Burkina Faso. With projections for Earth's population to rise another twenty-five percent over the coming thirty years, the rise in growing urban centers will only continue. By that time, Ouagadougou's population may reach five million from its 1.5 million today.

Although Ouagadougou would not qualify as a mega-city, it remains unclear whether growth from rural migration should be viewed with an optimistic or pessimistic eye.

The voluntary movement of people is called migration. This movement can occur either within the geo-political boundaries of a country or between countries. When conditions reach a point where tribal or ethnic unrest erupts from long dormant histories of distrust or from a hopelessly declining environment and political corruption, this movement becomes forced migration. Worldwide in 2012, the number of forced migrants is projected to have risen beyond fifty million people.

In many developing countries where there is little economic diversification, it has become more difficult for countries to remain politically stable and ensure opportunities for its people. As land quality diminishes and sustainable agricultural productivity falls, there will be a growing dependency on the importation of food and other commodities. Once established, the cycle between falling levels of food production and the decline in the health of a country's population is only likely to continue. With these declines, the need for increased healthcare services rises. These are all costs which poor, developing countries are little able to absorb.

This contrast between the urban character of Ouagadougou and the rural realities of village life provided the backdrop for an exotic experience in cultural diversity that became a reality check into the daily lives of some of Earth's bottom two billion people.

1. *Guard Your MoPed?*

Many young boys could be found living on the streets of Ouagadougou. They created an income stream that could actually be quite lucrative. Whenever Volunteers came to town, riding around on our MoPeds or in trucks, these boys would track you down, greet you and present their unique business opportunity to you. Everyone could be a winner!

They did nothing malicious and over time, we all learned to appreciate the service they provided.

Their service was simple but was not free. They were building a business and could not afford to give things away for free. Whenever you reached a destination and parked, a group of four to eight boys would quickly surround your bike and announce that they would guard your bike.

Guard it from whom?

It turned out that there was really no one to guard it from. However, their story was convincing enough to suggest that their services would be most beneficial. They ensured that no harm would come to each bike or truck that was protected. It was wise not to refuse a service that could be obtained for less than one cent – even if that meant one cent for each time you stopped!

The street-wise guardians marketed their services well and quickly proved just how important their services could be. One day, I tested the quality of their work by refusing their service. When I stopped to go to the market, I locked my bike with a cable. When I returned, the cable had been moved from the tire to the handlebars. The boys were quietly sitting on and standing around the bike.

I used their guard service each time I parked to ensure there would never be any vandalism to my bike. There never was.

2. Departure & Arrival

After a long trip from the United States – passing briefly through Dakar in Senegal, Monrovia, Liberia and Abidjan, Ivory Coast we landed in Ouagadougou. It was September and the end of the rainy season. The country had not been getting much rain, so there was also an absence of humidity. But it seemed hot – even at night. Burkina Faso rested halfway between the Atlantic Coast to the South and the Sahara Desert to the North. With the Sahel as its northern boundary, I soon discovered there would be too many opportunities to experience heat. Fortunately, it would be heat with very little humidity.

We were invited to the home of one of the teachers who worked with us throughout our six weeks of training in the Virgin Islands and who would continue to work with us for another ten weeks in-country. This provided me with a likely timeline for departure to my village.

We had fun "training" in the Virgin Islands and thought we had actually learned quite a bit of conversational French and even Mòoré – the language of the Mossi – the dominant ethnic group of the country. Oh, and it was in the Virgin Islands that we participated in our first well-digging training sessions. Just a couple of days were needed to declare our well finished after one of the daily tropical rain showers filled our one-foot deep hole with water. We unanimously agreed that our training had officially ended.

That statement severely underestimated the necessary training we were unable to appreciate that would lie ahead for us in Africa.

There were wooden benches placed around a mud-brick enclosed courtyard and we had the opportunity to meet many family members and Peace Corps staff. I was really in Africa! Whenever I closed my eyes, the sounds and smells became exotic. Whenever I opened my eyes, the sounds and smells became more strange than exotic. I knew my eyes would remain open during my two years as a Volunteer.

We were fed chicken and boiled millet. This again was another window into what I could expect after moving into my village. As I finished pieces of chicken, I asked my sponsor where I could throw the bones. He pointed to the vultures that sat upon the wall surrounding the compound. Throw your bones on the ground. They will eat the bones. Another cultural window popped into view.

I eventually began a final ten weeks of in-country training to even better prepare me for life in a village. It did not.

3. The Value of Experience

When I first arrived in Ouagadougou, its many sights and sounds overwhelmed me. Even though it was the capital, this urban center was unlike any city I was accustomed to seeing.

The behavior of people speeding on MoPeds through the streets made the capital seem much busier than any street I had ever experienced. These MoPed bikes and Peugeot trucks were remnants of a distant life in a former French colony. The MoPeds would perilously drive at open throttle throughout the streets. They rarely slowed down even for entering an intersection when they would just beep their horns to warn of their arrival. Trucks and cars would merely flash their headlights before making their pass through an intersection. These driving patterns made the streets quite dangerous.

The exotic smells and cacophony of strange new languages emerging from the giant, open-air, Central Market were even more overwhelming than this driving behavior. In time, these inherent dangers would disappear and become normal.

While having a beer at a local bar, I quickly learned about the long-practiced art of negotiation. After just one "training" session, I was able to buy a Rolex watch that could withstand a momentary dunk into a glass of cold beer and keep on ticking – for only US $10! It wasn't easy getting to $10 from a starting price of $50.

I questioned whether it was a REAL Rolex as well.

4. *Fashionable*

In the capital, everyone took traditional and contemporary fashion seriously. Or, maybe the change in culture just made it seem that way to me. Clothing could be represented by styles like Dashiki (for both men and women), boubous (long robes), and leisure casual shirt and pants.

Women donned fabulous prints and colors for batik clothes – the brighter, the better! Much of the clothing worn was tailored by one of the many shops in the city and the fabric was purchased right in the Central Market.

Of course, at that time, I was clueless to these fashion variations and just thought that everything seemed correct. The longer a Volunteer remains in a country, the more traditional the garb worn. Many times, traditional clothes were much easier to work in and to manage the heat than in our native jeans and khaki clothes.

For men, the robe of choice is the fugu. A fugu is widely used throughout West Africa. It has a rounded neck and short sleeves that have a rather wide opening. The smock worn in the bush is usually just white in color. From the waist on, the garb spreads in a funnel shape sometimes reaching ankle length. It has an amazing ability to keep the body comfortable in both heat and cold.

All of these could be seen in Ouaga. One fashion incident occurred during my first month in country. Feeling a bit more secure with my native language skills, I went into the Central Market to buy something and dabble in a bit of negotiation. I stopped a fashionably dressed young man to ask for the time. I had first checked his wrist to be sure he was wearing a watch. He was with the watch face facing down. This would be another important clue in appreciating the culture.

He was somewhat startled by my sudden request because without hesitation, he rolled his wrist to look at his watch. The watch face crystal was cracked and the watch had no hands. Without missing a beat he said that it was about 10 a.m. and moved away. The watch was being worn merely as jewelry. Prior to this encounter, I always thought that a watch provided current time. In our villages, only estimated time mattered.

This incident helped me begin to understand nuances of life in rural areas of the world's poorest countries. Time management is important but not so important that it can't be estimated.

5. The Airport

Traffic in the city was erratic and dangerous. There were very few traffic regulations that anyone heeded or enforced. Bikes abounded but MoPeds ruled. Shops of all kinds lined city streets. There was a five star hotel with a fabulous restaurant that served affordable meals much tastier than the steak/frites dinners eaten at one of the many more affordable African restaurants. You could expect to find almost daily entertainment from bands playing contemporary African music.

The expansive city was divided into "quartiers" – the French equivalent of neighborhoods. Diplomatic compounds with guarded gates and high surrounding cement block walls would be interspersed with "local" residences. The most obvious differences between the two types of residences were the building materials and guards.

Ouagadougou hosted one event that was unavailable anywhere else in the country. On any given Thursday evening, if you happened to be at the airport by 8 p.m., you could witness the once-a-week landing of a DC10 aircraft that was arriving from France. The main runway was just long enough to accommodate this enormous plane. There were at least two instances when the plane was unable to stop soon enough and actually ended up running off the runway!

Unfortunately, I missed both of those occurrences.

A naase
5

Travel

"Rapid and widespread changes in the world's human population, coupled with unprecedented levels of consumption present profound challenges to human health and well-being, and the natural environment."

Royal Society Report
"People and the Planet" (April 2012)

The cultural shift that Peace Corps Volunteers experience can be so dramatic that it is important to quickly establish a base of operations. As soon as a Volunteer moves into a village, a home should be created to provide a break from all of the new and strange sounds and conditions being encountered. Travel, just one dimension of this shift, can be both very exciting and very risky especially as a new Volunteer. After a cautious beginning, travel became a daily reality. It was only when traveling to a neighboring country that companions were recommended.

Several of us in the program lived and worked together in the same region within thirty miles of each other. We had trained together and were compatible enough to share many work and leisure activities. What became apparent to me very early in my journey was that this experience was not simply about my travels but about other travelers I encountered along the way.

Environment

I thought I was prepared for the uncertainties of living in Africa when I arrived in my new village home. The three-month transition period from arriving in country to arriving in my village was too abrupt to be called transitional. I was not prepared.

Simple things we often take for granted could easily become monstrous in scale. You did not go someplace without a reason. Whether by Moped, bicycle, on foot or by camel, travel could be treacherous – often masked by intrigue as well as fear. I always deferred to caution because that seemed to be the least dangerous option. For my two years as a Volunteer, it remained unclear – nor did I care to know what real dangers existed outside compound walls or closed doors in the cooler evening hours.

It was always necessary to remember that things are not the same throughout the country and taking uncertain steps in uncertain environments can take a psychological toll.

There were numerous contributing factors that caused Burkina Faso to be ranked as the third poorest country in the world. Being a land-locked, developing country with no direct access to coasts and ports posed a major problem. The lack of retrievable minerals or other natural resources was another. The drought in French West Africa at that time was the worst on record for the century and only worsened already challenging conditions.

Had I understood the implication of these conditions, it might have influenced my decision to accept a position in that country. I also did not understand the environmental implications that such a drought was having on water tables and the well process. There were few rain showers like those that occurred in the Virgin Islands' Training Center that could easily fill a one-foot deep hole with water.

Nor did I understand the implications of desertification and my contribution to this process. After all, I had just arrived and climatic changes are long, evolving processes where the relationship between humans and the elements slowly degrade. All of these things have been occurring for a very long time in this remote corner of civilization.

There were no factories spewing volumes of smoke into the atmosphere. But there were myriad small fires being used daily in the many villages and family compounds in the Sahel. The fuel needed to support the daily needs for cooking and for building was having an enormous impact on the amount of atmospheric aerosols being emitted – as well as on the amount of remaining vegetation in the region.

Recent research shows the enormous impact that the heat being generated by the Sahara and Sahel is having on global weather and even the frequency and severity of Atlantic tropical storms. Are these conditions the precursor to more hurricane Sandys?

As land degradation and freshwater availability continue to decline, there is reason for entire regions to consider adaptation options. Too often, the only real option is physical relocation. To those being displaced, this is not an acceptable option.

1. *Why Hurry?*

This was probably the most intriguing traveler I encountered as a Volunteer. He arrived at the Hostel one afternoon. He was probably in his late 40s or 50s and had the tanned and wrinkled skin of someone who spent a lot of time exposed to the elements. The element, in this case, was sunlight.

His journey began in Turkey, five years before. One day, he decided to leave his country to see other countries. The world was too large with too much to see and too many diverse cultures to experience. He packed a few bags with the barest of necessities and began his trip.

What made this particular traveler so unique was how he travelled. It was by bicycle! The bike he was riding was larger than any I had ever seen. The frame seemed much heavier and longer than conventional bikes. It just seemed to be designed for cross-country (yes, and cross continent) riding. It must have been sturdy because he was now in year five of his travels.

He rode from East to West across Northern Africa, then South along the Atlantic Coast to Ivory Coast and was now in Ouagadougou. His plan to complete the final phase of his journey was to continue East across the African continent to Kenya and return home to Turkey.

He said he was in no hurry to complete his journey.

2. *Time Off*

I decided it was time to begin seeing some of the country. My language skills were good and there were a variety of sites worth seeing further south in Burkina. I was invited to visit a Volunteer who lived in the town of Tenkodogo. The town is about 120 miles southeast of Ouaga. Travel time was estimated to be about 2 hours and 30 minutes.

That did not sound like a bad trip. Public transportation was my mode of choice. There was a central bus terminal in Ouaga that offered easy access to all travel routes. Departure time was scheduled for 1 p.m. It was suggested I arrive early to allow for "unexpected" delays.

I arrived early at 12:30 in the afternoon and sat around the terminal looking at the pool of travelers and entrepreneurs who provided such products and services as a shave/haircut, apparel and jewelry accessories. This was the variety of necessities any traveler might need for a trip. The commerce was brisk.

It was soon 1 p.m. and the bus sat idle and unoccupied. I inspected the bus and noticed that it had no window panels. It also used wooden benches for seating. Two and a half hours was beginning to feel like a very long time.

Nothing changed 30, 60 and 90 minutes later. No updates were available. The good news was that it did not seem like it would be crowded. By about 3:30 p.m., our travel group had grown to fifteen passengers. We were told that the driver was on his way and we could expect to leave within the next 30 to 60 minutes. Apparently, the original driver was ill and there were problems locating a substitute driver.

I let it pass. Those things can happen at any time. It was not until about 5 p.m. that our bus began loading with passengers. All cargo was secured on the roof. The bus comfortably held our group of thirty people. I know, I saw and I counted. By the time we actually left the terminal, the bus had mysteriously acquired another eight passengers. I know, I saw and I counted.

We had driven no more than five miles when the bus made a stop. It was at the home of the driver. He was getting food for the trip. Continuing for another several miles, we stopped again. Our driver – as were most of the passengers – was a Muslim and it was time for evening prayers. Each unrolled a small rug segment onto the side of the road, turned to face Mecca in the East and began to pray. I think this lasted for another fifteen minutes. Everyone returned to the bus and we were finally on our way. It was now about 6 p.m. Not too bad. We had gone about fifteen miles in just under four hours!

Trying to remain optimistic, I continued to suggest to myself that this could still be a reasonably quick journey since the highway between Tenkodogo and Ouagadougou was macadam.

Living close to the equator has its benefits. Daytime and nighttime are nearly equivalent – twelve hours each. Nighttime had suddenly approached. A few other stops were made to pick-up some other travelers. This was illegal but was a way for the driver to earn some extra money. Now the seating was really getting tight with these newest passengers lying across seated passengers. We now had forty-five passengers. I know, I saw and I counted. Predictably, this slowed our bus speed to just a fraction of the potential highway speed. It seems that the benefits of macadam were now negligible.

By 9 p.m., we went off-road to another bus terminal. The access road was dirt and filled with extra large potholes. Some passengers went into the terminal, while other, replacement passengers quickly filled their void. After just a few miles, the bus rolled to another stop. The driver discovered a flat tire. Everyone needed to leave the bus. Not only did he not have a spare tire, he also did not have a jack. Someone returned to the terminal for assistance. After what seemed like an hour, another bus arrived that we would take to continue our trip.

We were on the road again and it was now 1 a.m. My quick calculation put us at eleven hours and we had traveled nearly half of our route.

The travel sensation that had just settled in lasted for about one hour. We were again pulled over to the side of the road – this time by the police. They came to inspect the possibility that the bus was illegally transporting too many people! Imagine that! I think we then had forty-eight people. I'm not sure. I saw, got confused and probably counted wrong.

This must be a regular occurrence because as soon as the bus had stopped, a large number of passengers had quickly vacated the bus and headed down an embankment without being seen. They mysteriously returned after the police had left.

This time our rest was for nearly two hours. I think there were some serious charges being negotiated to compensate the police for allowing the bus to continue without issuing a ticket or fine. We began to move again and by 6 a.m. we were suddenly greeting the sunrise near our destination town – only sixteen hours later than I expected!

Since that marathon journey, I have not taken public transportation.

3. *The Encounter*

Riding across the lateritic soil was challenging for any vehicle. Camels definitely had an advantage and could make this trip a lot more easily and considerably faster than a motorcycle. The paths created by pastoralists moving their herds through the brush were often impossible to find or very often did not exist at all – for the uninitiated.

Camels were well initiated – as were the pastoralists responsible for creating this network.

For vehicles using the more conventional roads, the overused main routes could suddenly disappear from view into shifting gullies of sand.

Driving a MoPed through the bush was precarious. Flat tires abounded. When stopping to repair one of many flat tires from two-inch long Acacia thorns, flies immediately converged from nowhere to make the repair process more annoyingly difficult. Water in my plastic canteen was as hot as the seasonally hot, dry air that seemed to last the entire year!

Appearing on foot was a family of four – walking, very slowly along the side of the road. From their tattered, faded, blue-dyed "clothes", I knew they had arrived from far worse conditions in their southern Sahara home than were being experienced here. The under-nourished woman was carrying her even more emaciated child. We greeted each other with a nod and continued our journeys. Our cultures were too different to share more than a thoughtful glance. Everything between us was opposite.

During that week, I struggled with several more flat tires and finally returned to my village. I couldn't be sure those nomads ever reached their destination or returned to their home in the Sahara Desert.

I was very sure they were simply struggling to survive.

4. Lake Ferry

I had a fascinating ferry trip down Ghana's Lake Volta on the Akosombo Queen. Construction of the Akosombo Dam formed the lake that is the largest reservoir by surface area in the world and the fourth largest one by water volume.

There is a certain irony in the size and importance of this lake to both Burkina Faso and Ghana. The lake's headwaters arise from three river sources in Burkina: the Red, the White and the Black Volta rivers. Two of the three sources – the White and the Red are dry for five months each year.

Collectively, these form an important transboundary water system between the two countries. Yet, because the sources for the Lake originate in Burkina Faso, that country has guaranteed rights enabling it to divert water for national needs. Legally, this is referred to as riparian rights. Presently, most of the water extracted by Burkina is used to meet agricultural demands.

To Ghana, the main water of the Lake is used for hydroelectric power generation that accounts for nearly 75% of the country's total electric generation capability.

If too much water is withdrawn by Burkina Faso to meet growing national demands, the water level of the Lake will be lowered sufficiently to have a negative impact on the hydroelectric generation capacity of the Akosombo Dam.

I did not know about these issues when we travelled down the 320-mile length of the lake. But I now know that as environmental conditions become more challenging and population demands for water rise, disputes over water rights on all transboundary systems will only intensify.

I'm not really sure of how long it took to travel the length of the Lake nor am I sure about the beauty of the scenic views from our boat.

I spent most of the time dealing with the effects of dysentery. I'm sure you don't care to hear much about that part of the trip.

5. Ambition

During my two years in Africa, I met a lot of travelers with unusual stories. One American couple had driven a motorcycle from Spain, crossing to North Africa through Gibraltar, continuing down along the West African coast to Ghana before turning north to Ouagadougou. Because they were naïve in thinking this would be like an adventurous tour of Europe or the US, their travels came to an abrupt end when they eventually arrived in Ouaga – exhausted mentally and physically. Shortly after their arrival, they were flown back to the States unable to finish their romantic journey.

Two ambitious British guys left London nearly six months before to "explore" Africa. Quite different from the American couple, they actually had a plan. Flying to Capetown from London with little more capital than impressive – though fabricated – resumes. They were able to quickly get a job in a South African brokerage firm. It took the firm thirty days to discover the ruse.

Having only paper-credentials with no brokerage experience, they were fired. By the time of their firing, they had earned enough money to move to their next destination. They replicated this feat several more times. Burkina Faso was one of their final stops before returning to London – but not before covering six countries in five months.

A yoobe
6

Animism/Charlatan/Injury

"If there are to be problems, may they come during my life-time so that I can resolve them and give my children the chance of a good life."

Kenyan proverb

One thing I learned very quickly living alone in the remoteness of my African village was that illness was inevitable. Just as inevitable was the reality that somehow, it was possible to recover. Some illnesses had names too difficult to remember or pronounce and too exotic to wish for. Onchocerciasis – river blindness – was one such illness. Dracunculiasis – guinea worm disease was another parasitic worm infection that occurs mainly in Africa. As you can imagine, life in these remote villages was even more challenging for many of the local residents after generations of exposure to the many different parasites and diseases.

There were several types of very poisonous snakes – black mambas and vipers whose venom was extremely toxic to humans. Due to the lack of community medical services because of the country's economic challenges, homeopathic medical solutions far outnumbered the use of Western medicine. Many people knew about the first aid kit required for every Volunteer. When the presence of a medical kit was suspected and verified, proven traditional solutions suddenly became a distant second choice. There was just something special about the intense feeling of iodine being applied to an open wound.

You can be sure that injuries and general health issues abound – both to villagers and visitors to these distant locations. Some illnesses were so common that they became routine. These included malaria, dysentery, diarrhea and weight loss.

I have assisted many with health issues in Dablo and have been cared for more than several times by village elders. Only after leaving Africa have I discovered that there is another type of long-term health issue that is caused by humans tampering with the environment. It is pervasive land degradation. Humans are having a dramatic negative impact on the land's regenerative ability. This process of human-induced degradation, commonly referred to as desertification, is a never-ending cycle of the demands from increasing populations, agricultural production, grazing needs and woodlands/grasslands depletion.

Environment

Species thrive and species go extinct. This process is referred to as the natural extinction rate. Land degradation is becoming a form of extinction due to events in nature that are causing major changes to ecosystems.

Perhaps, the natural cycles of rising and falling global temperatures (whether they are 600,000 years cycles or two million year cycles) are the present cause of the world's receding glaciers? Perhaps, it is the decreasing levels of atmospheric moisture from this warming period that is the primary cause of the increased number and intensity of drought occurrences?

The similarity – a stretch – is based on the reality that the Earth as a tightly integrated symbiotic environment experiences constant motion and change. During the cycle of natural events – tornados, hurricanes, volcanic eruptions, change is inevitable. Over time, species experience lifecycle changes. Many survive. Many go extinct.

Land degradation, as an example, can have both natural and human causes. At some point, humans must realize that nature cannot be harnessed. We must learn to respect her power and be thoughtful about how and where we live in relationship to natural processes. As rising levels of atmospheric gasses continue to spew unabated from automobiles, factories and power plant generators, humans are intervening directly into the natural extinction process.

Land degradation degrades tradition as well. Ancient, proven homeopathic medicines come from specialized bushes and herbs. Traditional healers need specific ingredients to perform their rituals. The plants supporting these practices are disappearing quickly. Besides the impact of a changing climate, human intervention contributes heavily to this change. Both national and local governments are not proactive in taking inventory of plant needs and losses. Herbs, shrubs and trees, used to produce ancient medicinal solutions long practiced by healers and village elders are being depleted by environmental changes. I have only recently learned of the purposeful creation of botanical gardens in several West African countries to reintroduce and preserve the existence and propagation of important native species of trees and plants.

One afternoon, a man working for me as a mason said that he needed to go away for some time. He was not sure how long it would be and he was not sure where he would be going. He was asked to search for some medicinal plants for healing a sick relative. In years past, this was a simple task because the brush was thick and plentiful. He returned one week later not having found his plants.

Climate change is another area that has been transformed by human (anthropogenic) intervention. Excessive human contributions beyond natural processes are believed to have accelerated Earth's warming atmosphere. Human intervention and technological effectiveness have been rapidly depleting the planet of its reserves of natural resources from ocean fish stocks to forests of ancient trees.

It is estimated that the extinction rates today – those influenced by the actions of humans – are between 1,000 and 10,000 times higher than the natural extinction rate.

1. The Power of Spirit

The traditional healer in my village made a bold claim. He could create a medicine for me that would prevent injury and harm. If someone tries to stab me or cut my throat, the knife will drop from his hands! If someone puts poison in my drink, the liquid in the calabash will swirl around and the calabash will fall from my hands to the ground! He was fully confident of his claim.

To be effective, I had to be fully confident of his claim as well and believe that his medicine would guard me from harm.

When I first arrived in my village, I knew very little of and had no opinion about the animist rituals of the healer. I soon learned that he had quite a good reputation in this part of the country. I witnessed the impact of his power on neighbors more than a few times. Just being in the presence of a healer during one of his ceremonies exceeded my emotional imagination.

At one point in the ceremony, he would begin to sacrifice animals on his well-worn altar. Blood would be drained over the altar and over the "medicine" he was creating. Fully garbed in leather with long tasseled knives attached to his waist, his effectiveness was neither random nor accidental.

Eventually, even the healer knew I needed a cure for reducing the frequency of falling from my MoPed.

Driving throughout the bush was a mandatory requirement for the well-digging program. There was always reason to be searching for new well locations or to service the growing inventory of existing wells. Access roads to many villages seemed to be absent from view and could make navigation even more difficult.

Shifting sand from overuse was a problem with main roads. Protruding branches or remnant trunks from previously cut trees and bushes were regular occurrences with smaller roads. Precautions were also needed whenever I would overload the bike's rack or basket with food or well supplies. It was under those conditions that my bike became the most unstable.

There needed to be a proper balance between speed and weight with road conditions. I frequently overlooked this minor detail.

I decided I would visit the healer in my village. I was not surprised that his compound was cluttered with a variety of "essentials" to support his trade. I decided there were too many things to ask about. Besides, this was not a social visit. He knew I was coming and had something already prepared for me when I arrived.

The "gris gris" (medicine) was wrapped around the end of an animal's tail beneath a section of stitched leather. The leather was about four inches long and the tail segment was about twelve inches long. The leather was dyed with a common red color used on a variety of leather goods.

That was it! I would now be safe and fall no more.

I hung this prominently from the leather bag I carried daily. Surprisingly, the results lasted nearly two months. Did I stop believing in its power? Did I overwhelm its power with a lack of confidence? I kept the tail as a reminder of what is possible. The long-term benefits remain my secret.

2. *Little Men*

It did not rain very much during my two years as a Volunteer. When it did rain, the storms could be violent and the lightning, spectacular. Suddenly, the dry landscape would come alive. Lakes and rivers would appear where there were none before. Entire villages became isolated islands. Bullfrogs seemed to appear from nowhere and started croaking to each other. This often lasted throughout the night.

After a rain, the air became cool, even chilly. I discovered that after just one season in country, my blood must have thinned because what seemed like pleasant mornings in my first year, transformed themselves into cool, chillier mornings. By the second year, long sleeve shirts and pants were often required.

One evening during a particularly heavy storm, I was spending time with a visiting neighbor. I suggested we go out into the rain and cool down. The past several days seemed to have been particularly hot and even after this storm, there seemed to be very little relief. He wasn't interested.

During the storm, I continued to prod my neighbor into a quick walk in the rain. He refused to go. I thought maybe it was a fear of lightening. The light show from the lightning was especially brilliant.

No, it was not the lightning. It was the little men. When he finally explained this it seemed like this fear was yet another fable that had been so successfully passed down through so many generations that it had become true!

These little men are waiting for someone to walk outside into the night. They will approach the person and force an engagement. You must not talk to them, avoid eye contact and do not get into a fight. They fight until death. Yet, if you do encounter one of these little men and can keep them in a fight until sunrise, they will die. They must return to their holes before dawn or they will die.

I knew this was a tale that could not be validated. I also knew about the powers of a healer. I laughed each time I thought about this story, but I never took a chance to go outside for relief from the heat.

What if these little men were real? I was never really sure they weren't.

3. The Musket

Most villages come alive on market day. Maybe it is just the increased number of people congregating in market activity. Throughout Burkina Faso, local markets rotate on three-day cycles. That is, on every third day, markets will return to the villages in which they were held three days previously. This allows for a continuous stream of markets to operate without interfering with the economics of any single village.

Market day is a busy day for everyone in the village. My house sat on one side of the market square with its front door opening into the market area. Being the only white person in a twenty-mile range, everyone knew who I was and where I lived.

It was mid-morning and I was writing letters in my living room when someone knocked at the entrance to request my assistance with something medical. One disadvantage of not being fluent in a local language is the challenge of not understanding much of the context of any conversation. I tried to get as much information as possible but eventually, assembled what I thought might be useful necessities. Of course, this included my medical kit.

Several miles later, as we approached the mud brick hut of the injured elder, everyone backed away from the doorway to allow me access. Just for a moment, I began to feel like a doctor! I thought it might be important to know the cause of the injury. I was shown the remnants of his musket rifle that was made by a local blacksmith and used for hunting. The barrel of the gun had exploded in his hand and opened the large wound I was attempting to repair with my certified, Peace Corps issued medical kit.

The elder had his hand wrapped in several layers of cloth and supported by several folded blankets. I carefully unwrapped his hand and saw a rather long and deep-to-the-bone cut in the skin between the forefinger and thumb. Knowing that all similar rifles are made the same way, I cringed to think just how many hands might have suffered the same fate. At this point, fainting was not an option.

I asked for a calabash of water to soak his hand. All good medical kits provide a wash for abrasions. This was definitely more than an abrasion and appeared to be severe enough to fall into the category of "Not to be used on…" that drug manufacturers are required to mark clearly on the product labels to protect against frivolous lawsuits. I proceeded, knowing that lawsuits would not be an issue.

I soaked his hand for nearly ten minutes. His expression never changed. I knew he was in pain because of the perspiration that was beginning to run down his face. But he sat calmly, staring blankly in front of himself – imagining something far beyond my presence. Fortunately, I could not speak the language well enough to make small talk and bring him back to the present.

When I felt enough time had passed, I dried his hand and had to make a decision about my next step. I could either apply a topical antibiotic cream or iodine to the wound. Neither seemed appropriate. I chose the ointment and wrapped his hand in gauze.

I then explained that he should go to the clinic to have this temporary repair replaced with something more appropriate – like stitches. He debated and resisted the need for this next step insisting that he would be fine. I did as much as I could do and left.

Several months later, as I was walking through our market, I was approached by the man whose hand wound I had treated. He was smiling and thankful for my help. He showed me his hand, which was remarkably well healed. Perhaps this miracle had more to do with his visit to the infirmary where he received ten stitches than it did with my medical prowess. I accepted that reality and fortunately, was never needed again to perform such a repair. No longer a doctor, I returned to my role as a well-digger.

4. *The Black Stone*

There is a special stone that was first discovered in the Belgian Congo many years ago. That part of the story may be true because the stone can still be found today in the eastern part of the Democratic Republic of the Congo.

The next part of the story goes something like this. A Belgian missionary living and working for many years in the Congo somehow found a way to create a synthetic version of the stone. I discovered this synthetic version in a village market.

In French, the name is La Pierre Noire – The Black Stone. It has an amazing quality. Once it is applied to a venomous bite (snake or scorpion), the stone is able to remove the venom in minutes, healing the wound of the bitten person. Before using the stone, it must first be heated in what is referred to as the small black stone fire for about ten minutes.

The venom removal process can be repeated many times. However, each time the stone is applied to a wound, it loses some of its potency.

I carried this stone with me for nearly two years. In spite of the dangers of receiving a venomous – and potentially lethal – bite, I never needed to experience its powers.

A yopoe
7

Food/Nutrition/Drink

"On the most basic level, climate change has the potential to create sustained natural and humanitarian disasters on a scale and at a frequency far beyond those we see today. The consequences of these disasters will likely foster political instability where societal demands for the essentials of life exceed the capacity of governments to cope."

Admiral Dennis McGinn

Arriving in Ouaga was a discovery. Surprisingly, adjusting to life in the capital was not too difficult. There were good Lebanese food markets that offered both variety and quality. No meat was sold that had not been inspected. And, by having a full kitchen at the Hostel, it was always a treat to collaborate with a few other Volunteers in dinner preparations.

There was also a wide selection of local restaurants and clubs where you could get a reasonable meal with beer for

US$ 4 or 5. After nine in the evening, certain clubs would assume a purely French tone. The music found in local restaurants and clubs usually consisted of brass – lots of brass often six to ten horns, and electric guitars – usually three or four. The music was loud. The acoustics were non-existent and echoes abounded.

The French clubs by contrast were sultry and would always be well stocked with liquors. Lights were always low. Cruising around the clubs was a network of prostitutes – always willing to dance, share a drink and mingle closely with anyone there. You can decide what mingle might involve.

Village life bore little resemblance to life in the larger cities. Village work is hard. From about sunset to nine p.m., energy from the day is slowly released. The women have been preparing meals and caring for children while the men congregate into small clusters. Men and women do not eat together. The strange language sounds are like the bass and treble settings of a stereo. Eventually, the conversations taper to an end and all that remains is the smell of smoke from burnt wood and smoldering embers.

When all of the human activities and sounds have ended, the evening then belongs to the animals. The most vocal are the mules and roosters.

One of my "typical daily breakfast menus" might consist of a locally baked baguette, some oatmeal, eggs and coffee. I would often try to have a bigger meal for lunch than for dinner. I always tried to have some kind of meat (beef, lamb or goat), rice or pasta, and bread. While this diet helped me maintain a fairly constant weight, it was very constipating. I was always careful not to drink much caffeine or alcohol to minimize fluid loss.

Water consumption was a necessity. All water had to be boiled and filtered. It was a tedious process. Drinking too much water could also increase the likelihood of having some form of intestinal disorder. One male Volunteer attracted one of these disorders and continued to lose weight from his normal 220 pounds to 135 pounds before being flown to Germany for treatment.

We all found ways to survive these challenges. But it was our regular travel to Ouaga that made life just a little better.

Environment

The differences between my life as a Volunteer and life in today's world are too broad to even attempt comparisons. When I left for Africa, I was naïve in expectation. What I knew for sure was that I really wanted to use this as an opportunity for self-discovery – far away from the normal influences of home. I did not really know what that meant, but at the time it sounded good – and West Africa was definitely far away! One reminder I constantly raised was, if thousands of other Volunteers could stay and complete their two-year tours, then so could I. I do remember having to test myself frequently with this reminder.

Getting back to differences. Everything comes at a cost. When people lead a subsistence lifestyle, they are often only able to produce just enough to survive. My village neighbors were subsistence farmers. They had little beyond the basic necessities to survive a growing season. Rainfall determined what would germinate and grow to maturity. Rainfall even determined when ducks would lay their eggs!

One evening, I leaned over the mud wall between my compound and my neighbor's for a short conversation. I knew he had at least five ducks. I never saw anyone eat eggs or ducks. So, I asked if I could have the eggs. His immediate response was: "Mr. Tony, there won't be any eggs until it rains!" Six weeks later after the arrival of the first substantial rains came the eggs. My next lesson learned: ducks need ample amounts of water to form the calcium shells. Am I the only one who did not know this?

During mango season, the once barren-of-fruit markets would suddenly burst with mangos. There were so many mangos that within a few weeks of their arrival, my hunger for the fruit was gone. I can better appreciate the importance of seasonality.

As the global economy continues to assimilate more and more countries into its growing web, many people have begun to falsely believe that the planet can provide an infinite availability of food for consumption. Global markets have become conditioned into believing that there is no season for any product from any part of the world for delivery to any local market anywhere in the world.

We forget that there really is a season for every fruit and vegetable we find in our markets. The global demand to have whatever it wants, whenever it wants, from wherever it can be grown has created a complex network that is able to satisfy the need of anyone who has the money to make the purchase.

The future of global abundance can no longer be guaranteed and the world must now begin to think about the true costs of global availability, the constant pressure on land to maintain such productivity as well as the energy consumption required for transportation throughout this network. The implications of this complex network are endless.

Vast mono-crop, mega farms have evolved the global capacity to produce more food on one farm than collectively could be produced by all of the farms consolidated into the creation of one such mega farm. The supporting global transportation and distribution network for food defies imagination.

There are increasing dangers with such mega-farming methods such as the impact on soil quality and availability. Whether measuring the changes in topsoil depth or quality, the demand for constant food production is taking its toll. There is a famous series of photos from the early farming days in the San Joaquin Valley that shows the land surface has actually collapsed nearly thirty feet between the 1930s and 1990s. The massive Ogallala Aquifer beneath the Great Plains shows comparable losses from intensive water withdrawals.

Soil compaction occurs when soil particles are pressed tightly together reducing pore space between them. This is most often attributed to the use of larger and heavier farm tractors and field equipment. Further soil surface problems can been attributed to over-pumping of vast aquifer reserves.

The water held in an aquifer provides internal support for the soil around it. Whenever water is removed too quickly and nothing is put in to replace it, air remains to fill the void. Because air can be compressed, the internal structure of the aquifer can eventually fail and contribute to the collapse of the aquifer. Once the empty space collapses, the aquifer can never recover.

The world's two most populous nations, India and China have been irrigation-dependent on underground reserves for decades. Well depths have dropped significantly and today, less water is available for agriculture. As these populations continue to grow, the need to produce more and not less food will be needed. Further health problems can arise from greatly deeper wells. The concentrations of arsenic in the water get higher – beyond critical ranges for human consumption.

These conditions are arising on each continent. Countries that have invested heavily in this production technique are now showing signs of weakness. Vast acres of topsoil-rich fields have become compacted by the very equipment needed to harvest the crops. Even deserts can be turned into oases – but at a cost: as long as there is sufficient freshwater available to support such forced farming habits.

Saudi Arabia sits upon not just large, supplies of petroleum reserves but also atop one of the world's largest subterranean freshwater reserves – The Nubian Aquifer. In meeting with their strategic plan for food self-sufficiency, wheat production rose dramatically right out in the middle of the Arabian Desert. Not long after demonstrating this achievement, the program was halted. The Saudi's understood that it made little sense to plunder their most valuable underground water supply to compete with countries that had the natural resources for wheat production.

The Saudis understood that like peak petroleum, many parts of the world are also experiencing peak freshwater. The Nubian Aquifer was a more valuable strategic asset intact, deep underground than it would be if mined, depleted and sold to highest bidders in today's threatened freshwater market.

Irrigation dependency is threatening aquifer health and stability. Large mono-crop fields are threatening food supplies because of their vulnerability to damage that could destroy entire supplies. Inter-cropping is a much better alternative but not nearly as profitable. Businesses need profits. The world's financial centers like businesses that make profits.

Globally, water is already underpriced in many regions of the world. When something is free, its value is never appreciated and waste is often assured.

My village market was small. To a visitor, it would seem to offer little of interest or worth. Yet, even in the remote villages of sub-Saharan Africa, the true value of something is in its availability.

Eggs would come with the rain. In season, the availability of mangos was crippling. In many Western food markets, consumers have strong opinions about the quality of out-of-season fruits and vegetables that arrive daily.

Perhaps, in the not-too-distant future, the real availability of food will be less dependent on season than on who has the money to pay. As climate change begins to interfere with normal crop development, some food may not even be available to the highest bidder.

1. Does This Happen Often?

I had just moved into my first home. I was given the home of the previous Volunteer just because it worked for him. I sensed that by day two, this was not going to work for me. It was located on the outer edge of the village. Just beyond my compound were fields. It added to the feeling of remoteness and isolation.

I tried to settle in quickly but struggled with the isolation. Throughout the first week or so, a few men and boys from the village would come by the house, extend a greeting and stand by passively in my doorway for anything else that might be needed or said. I soon realized that my language skills were not quite as good as I had thought. There are only so many times you can say hello. Time didn't matter so questions about time were not important. You can see the trend.

Another Herculean challenge was sweeping a dirt floor. It can easily become a neurotic addiction. Often I just closed the door and sat in silence – collecting thoughts. Over the next few days, things did lighten up a bit. There were two school teachers in the village that spoke French that helped me navigate this new environment.

It was during this first week that I was working on something in the compound, when I heard a group of men yelling. Like the Doppler effect on sound, their voices would get louder and then softer and then fade away as they moved close to my house then quickly passed by – only to return again from the opposite direction. I glanced over the compound wall and saw what seemed to be a crowd of thirty men chasing after a dog. They had clubs and seemed intent on getting the frightened animal.

When I asked a teacher what was happening, he just casually said that the dog had rabies and the villagers were chasing him down to kill him so he would not be a health threat to the village! The "chasers" made one more pass and then all was silent again. The threat was gone.

2. The Power of Kola Nuts

Have you ever eaten a kola nut? They are very bitter. They make your mouth water. This is not something I would recommend. You can really get quite a buzz from a kola nut because they contain a lot of caffeine. To be honest, I think you would be crazy to eat a kola nut.

I'm surprised someone hasn't figured out how to make kola espresso! I have only seen red ones and white ones. They actually look like a very large Brazil nut.

I discovered that when riding a motorcycle for two hours across the parched roads of the Sahel, kolas became a special treat. Yes, they gave me energy but also created a natural canteen for my mouth – able to produce copious amounts of saliva!

In West Africa, kolas serve another important purpose. They can actually be considered a survival remedy for hunger. As the dry season ends and grain supplies are few, farmers must plant their fields for the following season. With less grain available to eat, there is insufficient nutrition for farmers' energy demands to finish planting fields.

Kolas nuts – eaten often – serve as a source of energy and hunger suppression by workers.

3. *How to Ferment Dolo*

Dolo is an indigenous alcoholic drink found throughout Burkina Faso. It could always be found in several locations on market day. And, once nicely settled into village life, I learned who made the "best" dolo. Armed with this information edge, I was able to avoid wasting unnecessary time tasting other uncertain quality brews. Yes, there most definitely are differences.

Sometimes it could be found on other days of the week as well. Only Christians drink Dolo, a traditional sorghum beer. Muslims avoid alcohol. To make dolo, it must be "brewed" and then allowed to ferment.

After being settled in my village, I had learned to distinguish the difference between good quality dolo from the bad. It was all about taste and not just about its alcoholic content. The dolo produced by the blacksmith's family was often the best.

Like any good beer, there is the need for a suitable fermenting agent. I watched the brew process a number of times and noticed that the yeast used to ferment the drink came in a small yellow packet. Coincidentally, these same packets of yeast were used by local bakers to bake bread. Something seemed strange about this process. Not that the yeast came in packets. There was something else that didn't make sense to me.

It made me question how a long proven traditional drink could have gotten access to small yellow packets of yeast to ferment the beer! Dolo, the national brew of Burkina Faso has evolved over generations. I began asking questions and unfortunately learned the answer.

The traditional method of fermentation – still actively used by many small villages – and the blacksmith's family – is an organic ingredient. It seems that the digested soil deep within the large, above ground termite mounds was the perfect fermenting agent.

Did I REALLY need to know the answer to that question?

4. *Eggs*

Whenever work on a well was begun in a village, the villagers would want to do something to show their gratitude. Sometimes I would be given a chicken or guinea hen. This was a premium gift that I would often not accept because of its importance to their meager subsistence living standards. That bird would be far more beneficial to their well-being than mine.

I did tell them that I ate eggs. They searched around for some but found only a few that they gave to me. They happened to be guinea hen eggs that are like quail eggs in size – half the size of chicken eggs. These did not survive the two-hour Moped journey back to Dablo.

My next visit to the same village was not for four weeks. We completed our work and I was ready to leave when they brought a small basket filled with guinea hen eggs. There must have been three dozen! Given their size, I guessed I might use six or eight in an omelet. I put the eggs in my refrigerator until the next morning when I decided to make an omelet for breakfast.

I heated a pan and without thinking began to crack eggs directly into the pan. The first egg was good. The second was good. The third had some remnant chicken embryo parts that had begun to grow. As did the third, fourth and then I stopped.

The eggs had been collected over four weeks and were at different stages of embryonic development. While I was ready to eat breakfast, I was not ready to study embryo development.

I was able to dissuade my friends from collecting any more eggs. It took me quite some time before I could enjoy a good omelet.

A nii
8

Knowledge of the Universe

"Don't go around saying the world owes you a living. The world owes you nothing, it was here first."

Mark Twain

Teaching about the universe may seem a little out of context with the role of a Volunteer. It was not for me. Once in a village, Volunteers begin the task of settling down. This included being introduced to as many neighbors as possible. Not that there were many to meet. Over time, I became less sensitive both to what I didn't know and their opinions of what I did know.

Although immersion is the best way to learn about any new culture, the learning process in this challenging environment requires the use of as many senses as possible. Two years were adequate for me to develop a functional understanding of language and customs. This was only possible with the help and patience of my new neighbors and friends. It's all about keeping things in a proper perspective.

Sometimes I got a bit too daring and took ideas into space where I became lost in explanation and they became confused in understanding.

Environment

I learned very quickly that what really mattered in my life was what was occurring at that very moment. Being in the moment. You might not associate that statement with the remote corners of the Sahel but for me, it took on a special meaning because death and illness were always in the area. I experienced more viral and bacterial infections than I even knew existed.

I used to think that the many bottles of liquor and beer found in restaurants and bars were to relax patrons. Those bottles also were consumed to keep microorganisms in check.

After being in country for a few months and finally acclimating to life in my village, it became a little bit harder a more of a nuisance to make that prolonged trip into Ouagadougou. Living in a remote village became soothing even though there were always dangers.

It was in the darkness of my village that I had an opportunity to really see the fringes of the Milky Way like I had never seen before. It stretched far across the entire night sky. In many places it looked like clusters of dust loosely scattered with dark empty spaces. The billions of stars were suns and our sun and solar system are just infinitesimally small components of the Milky Way galaxy!

The contrast between the jet-black sky and the clear, sparkling stars easily enabled my vision to come into sharp focus. The stars became my universe and my village was just one planet or asteroid floating around in the dark spaces between the stars. As you might imagine, I had some problems explaining our sun, our moon, and our planet to my neighbors.

From space, Earth appears as a mottled, blue marble, silently rolling around some central force. Try explaining that to someone who only sees a daily landscape that continues to decline in quality and where death silently waits.

Strong Harmattan winds from the East blow hot dry air in swirls for nearly six hours a day. This can continue for months during the dry season. With these winds come increasing incidences of eye, nose and throat infections that remain festering from the dirt-laden winds. Animals die from starvation as they futilely try to get any remaining nourishment from decaying baobab trees to substitute for morsels of no-longer-existent grains.

The Harmattan is just one of three major wind patterns that are influenced by the Sahara Desert. The others are the Haboob and the Sirocco. Together, these winds create a complex, three-dimensional impact on global climate. The heat from these African winds rise tens of thousands of feet into the atmosphere above the desert. As they come in contact with the higher-level atmosphere, they encounter jet streams that force their journey around the globe. The highest altitude winds travel north over Europe and begin their journey to Asia.

The strength of westerly surface winds moves dust-laden sediment from the African continent across the Atlantic. NASA photos and analysis have confirmed that there are critical links that have evolved from this relationship – from mineral distribution to South and Central America to the direct relationship between sediment levels on the surface of the Atlantic Ocean and the frequency and severity of Atlantic storms.

Atmospheric changes are reaching new proportions around the globe. Rising atmospheric heat levels are contributing to the evaporation of water in the reservoirs in the American Southwest. The moisture loss to evapo-transpiration is exceeding the loss from human consumption. Parts of Australia are only now beginning to recover from the impact of a twelve-year drought.

These conditions are no longer relegated to regions like sub-Saharan Africa but to high mountain ranges and drylands worldwide. Planet Earth functions as one, tightly coupled, network of ecosystems that are sharing each other's health and sickness.

1. *Vocabulary*

To really get into gear with language is to learn vocabulary. I found an old copy of an early effort of a dictionary to create the first written version of the oral, Mòoré language. I would carry it around because I thought it would assist me in asking questions more easily. African dialects are so guttural that there is only a slight similarity between the way it appears in print and its vocal form.

I discovered that using a dictionary was the most difficult resource for learning the Mòoré language. Simply sitting next to someone, pointing to an object and asking: what is the word for this? would get the fastest response with the least confusion.

One evening after dinner, I walked next door to visit my neighbor. He was Muslim and had just finished evening prayer. As the evening sky got darker, the display of stars in the sky was incredible. I pointed to the sky and asked for the word for star and then I asked for the plural. I was definitely on a roll.

When he asked if I had stars in my country, I answered yes, of course. We even have your stars in our country. He was amazed. I thought I would take another bold step in our conversation and began to draw some kind of picture of the earth and the stars in the dry ground. I thought it would be a simple task to just show how the earth and stars revolve in the sky.

The more I tried to explain, the more confusing my explanation became. I began to realize that I was only able to explain some form of Earth-centered theory of the universe. I began to understand the difficulty that Galileo had when trying to explain that the Earth is not the center of the universe and how his new view of the heavens would be considered blasphemy and lead to his imprisonment.

After that conversation, the universe remained as mysterious to my neighbor as ever but at least I had learned two new vocabulary words.

2. *Just a Matter of Perspective*

I met an Australian in a bar who, after more than a few beers, shared an interesting cultural detail with me. He proudly displays a map of the world in his office. What made this map special was that it clearly had an Australian's perspective.

Imagine! Australia sat prominently in the location and position of North America and the Northern Hemisphere was suddenly "down under" and turned upside down!

It made me wonder if the Sun is north or south of the Earth?

3. *Milky Way*

I always wondered how it was possible to see the Milky Way. I knew that clarity in the nighttime sky had more to do with urban lights and cloud cover than anything else. Once, I was settled in my village, I had more than enough time to really see nature – the Milky Way included.

This discovery also included some of nature's other ground-based critters such as scorpions, snakes and rodents. The latter were always chance encounters. Scorpions had a preference to move into stranded shoes while rats and mice would wait around until activities settled down for the night and then begin their walk around the compound in search of morsels of grain that might have fallen to the ground during meal preparation. Snakes successfully did whatever they wanted to do whenever they wanted to do it.

Well, that is not entirely true. I did witness one unfortunate snake that had an unexpected encounter with several women who were preparing grain for an evening meal. After seeing the snake emerge from the fence line of a village compound, the startled women went into prevention mode. As if a pre-planned response had been created just for moments like this, they got the wooden mortars they were using to crush the millet grain and began alternately hammering at the snake. Regardless of the venomous danger this viper possessed, it was no match for their instinctive assault. Each of the six times the snake was hit, its body would fly into the air as if rebounding from a trampoline. The women returned to work only when they were confident the danger had passed. That particular snake no longer posed a danger.

As the seasons rapidly moved from cooler/rainy to hot/dry, the opportunities increased for me to spend more evening hours outside my tin-roofed, mud brick house. I moved my cot-like bed to the rear of my house that was protected by mud brick walls, which provided some a sense of security.

It spite of the nighttime heat, a blanket was often needed to protect from the cooling evening air. The dusty rim of the Milky Way was even more pronounced because of the total lack of influence from the artificial light in the village or neighboring towns and cities.

It was not long before silently moving satellites could be easily detected. I knew that the stars visible to me in my village were just a very small portion of the stars that comprise our massive home galaxy. It also made me realize just how small I really was.

4. Orientation

I was talking with my landlord who lived directly next door to me. He was an extremely resourceful person. He worked very hard and was in such great physical shape. He resembled Evander Holyfield in every way. He could do things with his toes and feet that I struggled to do with my fingers and hands.

His attention was drawn to a jet flying in the sky above. Looking skyward, he stated with some certainty that my home was in the direction from which the plane was coming – north. And then he smiled as if he had broken some secret code. I could have said yes, and moved on but I said no, my home was over there, pointing northwest. He became confused. He looked at me and then at the path of the jet and began to justify his reasoning.

The airplane is white man technology. All white men live in generally the same area. I am white. Therefore, my home must be in the same direction that the plane was flying from. I understood his dilemma. I wondered how he would do trying to explain planetary orbits?

A we
9

Life in a Village

"We need to treat climate change not as a long-term threat to our environment but as an immediate threat to our security and prosperity."

John Ashton
UK Ambassador on Climate Change
to UN (2011)

Developing countries are becoming more and more challenged from causes that are often beyond village control. Life in villages is getting harder – not because of the work, but ironically because of the lack of work. Greater numbers of youth are leaving villages for larger urban centers because there is little opportunity to earn a living or a trade in the traditional rural setting. By far, the most significant industry in these countries is agriculture and/or is agriculture-related.

Increasingly, as climate changes have brought changes in temperatures and rainfall patterns around the globe, developing countries in the warm and tropical regions are being even more impacted.

Sub-Saharan Africa has suffered with severe drought cycles throughout much of the 20th century. In the late 60s and 70s, the countries of the Sahel suffered the worst drought of the century. That pattern continues virtually unabated today.

Village life is a delicate balance between the need for fuel wood and building materials; purposeful land and water regeneration programs (improvements in health, sanitation, and water systems); and declining standards of living and natural resources. Greater quantities of aerosols are contaminating homes and atmosphere because of the ever-rising dependency on scrub trees and bushes for use as fuel wood. Soon, those fuel sources will depleted.

A visit to any small village scattered across the Sahel will validate the impact from climate change, uncontrolled population growth, and degrading environment.

Environment

Life in villages throughout the developing world is challenging even for domestic pets. I use that term carefully because I do not believe there are any pets in villages. There are guardians from predators who become predators whenever necessary and frequently become prey. Nothing is ever wasted. The utility chain drives deeply from elder to child to guardian to pet. Everyone in between has an assignment – regardless of age, or of competency or of species.

Dogs and cats have obligatory guardian roles. Food is thrown to them whenever an owner has a bit to give. The dogs must keep vigil over compounds from anything foreign that might try to enter. Cats protect from rodents and snakes. Performed correctly and they survive one more day. The tolerances for mal-performance are razor thin.

After each harvest, the fields are slashed of any remaining growth. Useful biomass that can be feed for animals is removed. Fires are then used to rid the fields of any remaining and useless growth – perpetuating a cycle of rising atmospheric aerosol levels. Nothing is mechanized. Clearing a field is just one more manual task that awaits men, women and children of all ages. This is tradition.

I passed a field with a lone laborer. It was late in the afternoon and his well-conditioned body was shirtless under the cooling sunlight. He had a dabba over one shoulder that he used as an axe whenever necessary. Like virtually everyone, shoes were not ever needed because the bottoms of their feet were as cracked and hardened as the sharp, lateritic soil that made the ground look like some ancient lunar surface.

We greeted each other and he took water I offered from my canteen. I continued to my village.

When mentioning this to one of the teachers, he said he knew the family. That was the grandfather! I thought he had to be no older than 45 or 50 years old and he was probably 90.

This close living with the land has enormous benefits that far transcend any school learning. It is this traditional knowledge that begins to erode when the temptations to leave a remote village for a large city increase. Elders know that they have little control over the environment. And, when more than 65% of a country's economy is agriculture-based, they can only sit under the shade of trees and wait for things to change. Nothing ever does.

New vocational training is required to provide skills beyond agriculture. In a country where roads simply disappear during use or flood heavily during seasonal rains, it becomes quickly evident that there appears to be other more pressing needs that obviate any plans to raise the skill levels of women and youth. As climate changes, the worse becomes worst. Eventually, worst must find new words to describe this new degree of worseness.

Under these extreme conditions, life continues to move forward. Whether villages are recipients of new, concrete wells to replace traditional wells that have collapsed, those who live under the most extreme conditions will somehow find a way to continue to survive under even worsening conditions.

Ironically, to me at least is that those who become more vulnerable are those who believe they are exempt from these conditions. They suspect something is wrong but because they are fortunate enough to be driving a cab in Ouaga, they can afford to speculate on the causes without too much about the consequences.

This becomes even more obvious when you realize just how quickly the flash of a disease can take the lives of children before moving silently to a new destination.

1. *Salt of the Earth*

It was a later-than-usual morning to begin activities. After a grueling six hour return trip from Dori, I had barely made it onto my stick-frame bed and closed the mosquito netting when it was time to rise. On very hot days, it was best to rise before 6 a.m. A lot can be accomplished between six and ten in the morning. What has not been completed by midday must wait until late afternoon or another morning. The afternoon hours are spent in the shade of trees engaged in conversation or catching any momentary passing breeze.

On market day, it is the sounds from the surrounding market that are normally my wake-up call. I was still very tired and struggled to get out of bed.

The early sounds coming from the market today seemed different. I put some water on for coffee and opened my front door to greet the morning and the market. Today was very different: the people, the sounds and the smells. Walking from my house into the market and glancing around the crowded market area, I saw about fifty camels! Camels are rarely seen this far south from the Sahara Desert.

This caravan was laden with large slabs of ground salt that had been quarried from ancient salt pits in the Tenere Desert region of Niger. This mining tradition dates back thousands of years. But change has been slowly underway throughout this hot, dry region of Africa. Transportation by truck has become the mode of choice throughout most of the Sahara Desert and northern Sahel. Although a camel caravan is perceived to be less costly and more efficient in many ways than by truck, trucks are able to make many more trips to and from the quarry and to make considerably more money throughout the quarry season. This change has taken yet another cultural advantage away from the long-feared Tuareg nomads.

These salt caravans occur in the autumn by the Tuareg who use the mineral to barter for millet, beans, maize, cheese and dried vegetables.

Today, a small caravan of Tuareg has stopped in Dablo. What I notice immediately about the women is an overtly ostentatious ornamental display of silver jewelry. It is woven in the hair, hung from the neck as chains and dangling from wrist as bracelets. However, even more dramatic and visually obvious is the indigo blue color stains on lips and hands. It comes from the blue clothing they wear. From this pigment, they have acquired the name of "Blue People". Only a few of these nomads were curiously fascinated by the "White Person" who suddenly appeared in the market.

By mid-morning, awake and fully organized, they left the village as silently as they had entered.

2. *He's Just a Cab Driver*

One day in Ouagadougou, I was having a conversation with a cab driver while taking a taxi across town. When he discovered I was a new Peace Corps Volunteer, he became very animated and began asking me a lot of questions. Some were pretty basic. There was this one thought, in particular, that he wanted my opinion – something he had been thinking about for some time. It was about the changing weather in his country. He had a theory about why the temperatures seemed hotter and rainfall was more sporadic and unpredictable.

He believed that countries sending rockets into space were causing the changing climate in his country and the region! He didn't name names but I knew he meant Russia and the United States. These rocket launches were somehow damaging the atmosphere. What did I think of his reasoning?

At that moment in the cab, I began to smile at his naive theory.

Today, I smile at his prescient wisdom.

3. *Climate Change*

There is continuing debate about whether or not climate change is real.

Yes, the Intergovernmental Panel for Climate Change (IPCC) has made some recent errors in an apparent cover-up of internal scientific exchanges that made the international organization of climate scientists appear to be hiding or confusing the truth about climate change data. It was believed that those facts, if available to the public, would show that climate today is stable and that any variations are not anthropogenic anomalies but simply natural causes.

Whether the naming preference for the shifts in global weather conditions and extreme weather pattern changes is to use "changing climate" versus "climate change" has become a moot point.

> There's something happening here
> What it is ain't exactly clear
> There's a man with a gun over there
> Telling me I got to beware
> I think it's time we stop, children,

what's that sound
Everybody look what's going down
There's battle lines being drawn
Nobody's right if everybody's wrong
Young people speaking their minds
Getting so much resistance from behind
I think it's time we stop, hey, what's that sound
Everybody look what's going down
What a field-day for the heat
A thousand people in the street
Singing songs and carrying signs
Mostly say, hooray for our side
It's time we stop, hey, what's that sound
Everybody look what's going down
Paranoia strikes deep
Into your life it will creep
It starts when you're always afraid
You step out of line, the man come and take you away…

For What It's Worth
Buffalo Springfield

4. *Know Your Options*

It is not easy to distinguish one town from another in the Sahel. They all have little or no vegetation. They may have a concrete block school – constructed from funds donated by an international organization. Or, more likely, a few government facilities also constructed of concrete block. All remaining buildings will be made of mud brick. There are a few "roads" between large towns to accommodate traffic that is primarily trucks and busses. I often thought of them as "floating roads" because over time and with use, roadbeds turned into sand and needed to be rerouted to facilitate travel.

Primary roads are not nearly as necessary as the numerous random, meandering "secondary" roads and footpaths. These are the real channels of life most often travelled by pastoralists on their evening grazing walks; by women and children walking to and from village wells; and by bikes taking the most direct route between small villages.

As you approach a town or village the one noticeable characteristic might be a building cluster or the skeleton of a marketplace. You can tell you have reached the market area because it will probably have the largest cluster of trees. And, where there were no trees, there would be purposeful pole clusters to support stick mats that provide extra pockets of shade to the merchants. The poles were standard equipment in the market. The mats were strictly BYO – Bring Your Own. Commerce needs shade to be effective.

Regardless of size, market day brings life to a village, even in the most remote corners of the Sahel.

When I arrived in Djibo, it was not market day. The tree clusters were so few, that I could not even locate the place where a market would be if there had been one. Ironically, I was able to locate the strategically placed bar/restaurant. Yes, in spite of there being no trees or definable market, you could expect to find some place to get a drink. Drink options were few – either Johnny Walker Red, Dimple, Heineken, or Coke. Don't touch the water and <u>never</u> use ice in spite of the heat. Stomach disorders abound. I could never decide what was worse – dysentery or malaria. I'm still not sure.

What is really cool about any hyper-arid location like the Sahel is the lack of humidity. When there is little or no humidity, there is no condensation on the side of a cold drink bottle. That is a weird experience – a cold bottle but no sweat. Notice how easily a mind can wander to or from important details. Bottle condensation was usually the least of anyone's problems trying to navigate this sparse region.

When I walked into the bar, a single table was occupied and to my surprise, it was occupied by three other white men! Usually, seeing just one white person at any time is enough to create a crowd so you can imagine I was more surprised to see this group of three than they were to see me – and they were very surprised to see me. They invited me to sit with them and bought me a drink. They were French.

Our conversation got serious but not complicated. They wanted to know why I was there. I had the very same question for them. They were shocked that I lived in the area. I was shocked that they were going to cross the Sahara Desert by truck to return to Marseilles where they lived and worked as auto mechanics.

I guess in their minds, they could resolve any mechanical failure experienced during the desert crossing. In my mind, I could survive my two years in the Sahel.

I am not convinced they safely crossed the Sahara. Tuareg camels survive quite nicely without mechanics.

I think I am right.

5. Be Prepared

There was little value to wasted opportunity – especially in such a resource poor environment as the Sahel. Virtually, nothing was wasted. When something was finally discarded, you can be certain it had no further utility.

While passing through villages to inspect two wells, I came upon an elderly man walking alongside the road. This type of encounter is very common and often happens many times a day. It was hot and the time of year when fields were cleared of remaining crop growth. Some of the smaller growth was burned. The larger growth, such as millet stalks, were collected and reserved as supplemental food for animals. During a period of drought like was being experienced in the early 70s, there was little opportunity to waste even the smallest morsel of food.

This elderly man was carrying a very large bundle of dried millet stalks upon his head from his field to home. I stopped to take a photo. He also stopped to allow a photo to be taken. His willingness surprised me because superstitions abound and often permission to take a photo is not always granted.

He was wearing a traditional fugu and had a musket strapped across his shoulder. As he proceeded to drop his bundle to take advantage of this rare photo opportunity, he was distracted by a small cluster of guinea fowl just off the road. These birds are very noisy and are also very tasty.

He pulled his rifle from his shoulder and began loading it with gunpowder. When he realized he did not have any shot, he searched the ground and found a handful of small stones, which he quickly packed into the barrel. Once packed, he carefully aimed at the still present birds that were just a short distance from the road and pulled the trigger.

There was a very loud noise from the exploding gunpowder and an even larger cloud of smoke. When the smoke cleared, there were no dead fowl. The noise frightened them to move a few yards further away but they continued to feed as if nothing had happened.

The elder picked up his bundle and continued home. The guinea fowl continued grazing, safe for another day, and I moved along to my destination.

At least I was able to get a photo.

6. *Swimming Partners*

After spending a year living in the hot, dry northern regions digging wells, we decided to take a small vacation to the more tropical southern city of Bobo Dioulasso. Bobo was once the capital of the country. Another volunteer lived there and during our visit, we were invited to swim in a local tourist attraction – Banfora Falls. We had very few pools of water in the north. If there were any, we would certainly not swim in them.

This was a treat. To see the waterfall was invigorating. To be able to swim in the pool beneath the falls was even more invigorating. Living high among the crevices of the rocky wall were large populations of baboons. They stayed high and stared down at the pool of swimmers. We stayed low and cautiously watched their uncertain behavior.

We had also bought some fishing line and hooks. Eating fresh fish would be more than fantastic! We never caught any fish. However, as I fished the shoreline of the stream that exited the pool, I noticed something move in the water. It seemed so slight that I wasn't sure I had seen anything at all. It reappeared then disappeared again. I left the bank and told the others.

One of the others said he had bumped into a rock in the middle of the pool. We dismissed both the "rock" encounter and the sighting.

When we told our friend of our afternoon she confirmed that we probably had met some of the pool resident hippos!

We had been in the water with hippos! It seems that they leave the pool when the sun has set and the land begins to cool to graze on fresh grasses. They leisurely return to the water early in the morning while the air is still cool. They were not grazing when we were swimming.

7. The Camel Market

A visit to the hot and even drier-than-Dablo northeastern city of Dori was a very different experience from the region around my village. Just getting there from my village was a challenge. It took about six hours on MoPed. There was only one main road and numerous small, pastoral pathways between small towns along the route.

I got lost several times. The further north I travelled, the fewer people spoke Mòoré or French. Surprisingly, I did meet two people who spoke English from their time living in Ghana. I eventually arrived. Dori is considered the capital of the Sahel region of the country and is predominantly Muslim. The residents are Fulbe. The language is Fula.

I was definitely out of my element.

It was market day and unlike any I was accustomed to seeing in the region around Dablo. Camels were spread throughout the market. The merchants brought their wares to sell strapped to the backs of these desert ships. Camels are not polite and do not like human contact. I was having a problem trying to make trivial camel contact. We respected each other's preferences by avoiding the unnecessary.

I thought I was prepared to negotiate for something – anything. Eye contact is an immediate opening to begin discussion. The item being sold is irrelevant. They want your money. I passed one young merchant and noticed an interesting carpet on the saddle of his camel. I hesitated a few seconds too long. His friend approached me to ask if I saw something I wanted to buy. I said no and walked away.

Each time I passed by, they would jump out to engage me in a sale. Each time I refused. After about an hour, I finally shared that I may be interested in the carpet on the saddle of his camel. He immediately asked me how much I would offer. I started low with a power bid of $2. He was offended and responded with his power bid of $400.

After on and off again discussions over the next hour, the price narrowed. To justify his high asking price, he shrewdly suggested that he thought I wanted to buy his camel. He was only willing to lower his price further when he thought that I REALLY wanted to buy the saddle.

I eventually purchased just the rug for $15 and still I think I paid about $10 too much.

8. *What If He's Right?*

For two years, we battled heat, illness and cultural strangeness to provide sources of clean, fresh water to traditional villages in one very small part of West Africa's Sahel.

We weren't unique – though the experiences were unique to each of us. The projects were more than just symbolic. In our new world, they rivaled, in significance, any international aid program. Some volunteers stayed for another year, or two; some stayed for three years and some stayed much longer.

For me, it was time to leave.

I sat in the city's upscale hotel dining with a World Bank representative who was visiting the region on a planning assignment for yet another aid program that the Bank does so well. At some point, we began to discuss my program. I proudly offered an account of what had been accomplished while spending two long years in a remote village, during one of West Africa's worst drought periods of the century.

The representative listened attentively. I was waiting for his acknowledgement of my success. There was none. In spite of all we discussed, one question the Bank representative asked continues to resonate many years later. "Would I consider that perhaps by digging a well in one of those remote villages and providing a cleaner and more stable supply of freshwater might actually be contributing to spiraling environmental degradation by keeping villages alive just a little while longer?" To me, although I did not realize it at that time, this was an early clue to the impact of population on the health of the environment and a major cause of desertification.

Could a well deliver false hope with its clean, fresh, water?

9. 400

The number 400 may not seem to be any special number. It is not. But it does have special meaning for me for it relates to a shocking reality of life and death in the bush. It occurred in my village and its surrounding region.

The region supported both pastoral and sedentary groups. Besides obvious physical feature differences, other lifestyle distinctions between the two groups were very evident. Sedentary groups live in villages. By nature, pastoralists are always moving their animals to fresh grazing areas. To protect themselves from temperature extremes, they wear heavy cotton robes with long open sleeves. The sleeves can be rolled back over the shoulders during the day if it gets too hot.

They live in stick frame, mat-covered homes that can be easily assembled and disassembled. In good times, they share water from village wells. They are on the move so often that the small trails worn through the brush come alive from this constant movement of cattle, sheep and goats.

When conditions are favorable, their presence in the market is visibly noticeable. Pastoral women are able to generate income from selling dairy products. They keep the profits from all sales and often invest in ornate, gold jewelry as assets. Their assets are conspicuously worn every day.

The younger girls (women) have not yet developed their business skills but will still adorn themselves as much as possible with hair braiding, copper earrings and bracelets. The children are more inquisitive than their elders. Occasionally, a few would come cautiously to the front door of my house just to see the stranger.

There was one memorable group of three sisters. Their visits were very sporadic and unpredictable. Upon arrival, they always stood in the doorway of my house but would never enter. Wisdom at such a young age. They never really wanted more than to just look. I had some butter cookies that I thought they might like. I knew it was not like anything they would ever get on their own.

I opened the small packages and gave one to each sister. After looking at each other for some time, they took a cautious bite and immediately spit out the strange tasting food.

My efforts at creating a cultural bridge were shattered.

A few months later, it was time for our monthly supply trip to Ouagadougou. Usually this trip was made by three or four of the well-diggers who lived and worked closely together. We were gone for about six days – a bit longer than usual. Several markets came and went after my return to my village and the three sisters had not returned for a visit.

I was speaking to a friend about this and he told me that while we had been in Ouaga, a measles epidemic had spread rapidly through the area. There were many adults who had died but there were about 400 children who also died.

That is how life and death coexist in remote villages of the developing world.

400 is not any special number. But to me, it was shocking that 400 children who lived so silently could disappear so quickly. I was never able to confirm that the disappearance of the three sisters was due to the measles, but they never again returned to my doorway.

10. Special Reunion

I had arrived in Foube by mid-day to visit with the chief and discuss the village well. This would be more of a progress report since the well being dug had been ongoing for about two months. Foube lay at the farthest point of my assigned region – about two and half hours by MoPed. We were about ready to begin construction of a school within walking distance of the well. The site had been chosen by a small village council. This proved to be an important endorsement.

The chief was busy so I was escorted to a nearby house. Once inside, two men speaking Arabic immediately greeted me. I knew this was going to be a very long afternoon. Imagine three people in a two-language conversation. I spoke French to one who then spoke Arabic to the other.

The two friends were on their way further North much deeper into the Sahel. They left Abidjan months ago and had been travelling by mule. Apparently, one of them had a son nearby who he was trying to rejoin. They had been separated for nearly two years. He had a thought. Would I be willing to drive him on my MoPed to meet his son? He thought the trip would be much faster than to continue by mule. I thought the trip would take no longer than a few hours.

He could rejoin his family, get two camels and return for his friend. These two were definitely not mule men. They were camel men!

Not having anything immediate on my calendar, I agreed. I filled my canteen with water and we headed north. What I expected to be a short trip ended up taking us about five hours. There were several crucial mistakes made in calculating the length of time for the trip. Our mode of transportation was the first.

Camels travel in a straight line. They create roads where there are none. Thorns do not interfere with a camel's progress. In fact, the thorns of the Acacia tree are a delicacy to the hardened mouth of a camel. Those same thorns will penetrate an air-filled tire at will. The five flat tires we incurred were definitely a problem.

Getting lost numerous times caused several other delays. It is not so easy tracking down a pastoral group in the random countryside of the African bush. To my surprise, some people had actually seen his son and guided us in the direction of their location. Suddenly, with darkness fully in place, we came upon a cluster of rounded mat huts and burning fires. That was a good sign to my companion. I thought that if he was happy then so was I. The sighting proved to be true. The encampment belonged to his son.

When the father and son finally connected, it was a very emotional moment. The son appeared to be only about fourteen years old but acted many years older. He said that the return of his father was a very special event so we would have a special meal of lamb.

As the lamb slowly cooked, we remained seated under the open evening sky for another several hours. The difference in the darkness of the land and the black evening sky became indistinguishable. It was the sparkle of the stars and burning fire embers that grew stronger and provided the few glittering spots of light. The lamb was cooked by laying the pieces directly onto the burning firewood – only salt and ashes seasoned its taste. Three cups of tea were served.

It was not long after that I fell asleep under a blanket beneath the stars. Although the nighttime air was cool, I was quite comfortable and the morning came quickly. Again, in the morning, another round of three cups of tea was served. This tradition dates back to customs of the Maghrebi and Berber of North Africa. Not only is tea served at mealtime, it is also commonly served whenever there are guests.

Each of the three servings has a special meaning. To avoid insulting a host, the three cups must be drunk at the same sitting. There is no rush to complete this three-step ritual. Both the company and the tea are meant to be savored and enjoyed. Children are only permitted to drink from a sweetened fourth cup.

That morning, after tea, the father had one more request. He always wanted to drive a MoPed. "Would I let him drive my bike and he would let me drive his camel?" It sounded like a reasonable request. He went first. In spite of his confidence, I could tell that he had never done this before. But it was too late. He immediately opened the throttle and bolted across a field strewn with holes and jagged plant stubs. He was bouncing up and down on the seat and was barely able to turn off the gas and stop. I had a strong vision that I would be living with these nomads as a permanent guest!

I mounted the sitting camel by stepping on his neck and putting one leg over a leather saddle. Camels do not like humans. He began to hiss and groan. Suddenly, its body shifted to rise – first with its hind legs then to its front legs. The rocking motion felt like being on a boat in an angry sea. I pulled on the reins and he started to walk and then run. I was bouncing up and down on the saddle as my friend had done on the seat of my MoPed. Did I look as bad to him as he did to me?

It was not long before I had ridden far enough. I dismounted the camel and eagerly walked towards my MoPed. We both realized that we preferred our traditional modes of transportation. I returned to Foube in only a few hours. I somehow managed to avoid thorns and flat tires. By the time my nomad friend returned with fresh camels to replace the worn mules, I would be home ready to enjoy a quality night's sleep on my stick-frame bed and straw mattress.

A piiga
10

The Well

"You are not stuck in traffic. You are traffic."

TomTom
Satnav Advertisement (2010)

Just as the market holds a prominent spot in the life of a village, wells are just as important – if not more so. When I saw firsthand the consequences of wear and tear on a traditional well, it became clear that these holes in the ground that are the lifeline of villages can also be very dangerous.

As more and more people use a well and more water is extracted, the wellhead opening begins to deteriorate. It could be from the water being extracted that often drips from the calabash or bucket making the ground soft and muddy. There may also be visible signs of rope "burn" on the soil. As children are less able to safely lean over the hole to draw water, they will often sit down next to the well pulling on a rope. These actions eventually wear away the well-head. In time, it is not unusual to see large, gaping holes of six feet in diameter or more. The water retrieval process then becomes even more perilous as villagers must construct a maze of wooden supports along the inside of the widened well-head to support their climb down deeper into the well to access the water.

I discovered many years later that – contrary to what I long believed – there are even more significant consequences for providing cleaner, more permanent wells to regions, like the Sahel. Besides causing greater degrees of soil degradation, those regions will begin to experience greater natural resource depletion.

A permanent well will convey a false sense of security to residents of the village. In spite of the continuing drought, there may always be a supply of water. This false security justifies remaining in their villages, extending their search for fuel wood, deeper and deeper into the neighboring countryside. With little chance to regenerate, land can become permanently useless.

Environment

I have always been fascinated by a well. Looking down into a deep hole was like trying to visualize the boundary between rivers of water flowing beneath my feet and the hard earth that sat upon them. Nothing really flows – as in the sense of a river. But once a source had been tapped, it could provide "free flowing" water for many consecutive hours. You could tell how good a well was by the activity around the well. Lots of people suggested lots of water.

All wells were hand dug by usually two men in the well at the same time. Some wells were much easier to dig than others. Some would require driving mining bars through three to five feet of bedrock. If the diviner who was used to select the placement of the well said there was water below, then even slabs of bedrock were unstoppable. Standing at the bottom of a shallow well was almost like standing above ground. The deeper you dug into the earth, the cooler the surrounding air. If you hit a flowing stream, you might be constantly standing in three feet of water!

That was the idyllic part of the task.

Imagine being sixty feet below ground and having tools or a rock falling from the bucket transporting materials to be discarded to the surface!

There is often a lot of politics in the site selection of a well. A village chief or a healer might insist the well be dug close to their compounds. The best site was always the one most available to the most people such as near the market. Once a decision to move forward was made, everyone assumed a necessary role.

The women were responsible for gathering baskets of small lateritic stone that would be mixed into the cement. Children would bring back buckets of sand. There was never an absence of sand. Piles of material would begin to collect near the site.

Concurrent with this activity was the arrival of the diviner. The better known he was to the villagers, the more credibility he had and the more labor would be expended to fulfill or dispel his predictions. Once this well site was identified, it was time for a Volunteer to take part in the process by scribing a circle into the soil at the exact location selected by the diviner. At that time, the first instructions were given to begin digging. It's not that the men needed instructions on how to dig a hole in the ground. But they did need to stay within some very specific boundaries to ensure that the cement well wall would be neither too thin nor too thick.

The remaining activity was simply hard work. A typical well was about six feet in diameter with an average depth of fifty to sixty-five feet.

1. Mule in the Well

We spent the morning digging the well within sight of the healer's compound. This well would not be deep – maybe fifteen feet. More important than retrieving deep water with this particular well was providing a clean, permanent source of freshwater. There were numerous traditional wells surrounding the compound easily distinguished by the size of the ever-expanding well heads. Constant retrieval of water, wind and sporadic rainfall would gradually wear away the perimeter of the hole until it appeared to be a large, open pit.

There was a lot of commotion as I was pulled to the surface of the well. People were running towards the location of one of the large open pits. When I arrived, I was shocked to see a young boy still sitting on a mule. Both had walked too close to the opening and had fallen into the well. The boy was unharmed. The mule was simply dazed. Even the mule understood that this was just not a place for him to be.

The boy was pulled from the well and ropes were secured around the chest of the mule. Minutes later, the mule stood quietly alongside the ominous hole. He was obviously stunned to have fallen into the well and just as stunned to have been quickly removed from the well.

The healer arrived, quickly cut-off the tip of the mule's ear and threw it into the hole. His medicine must have been effective because I never again witnessed another mule-in-the-well incident.

2. Searching for Water

The advice we were given was that in order to better engage villagers in the well-digging process, a resident "diviner" should be used. He brought credibility. I just brought supplies.

The first time I used him to find the right location to dig a well was my very first well on the grounds of the local school in Dablo. Like the rest of the landscape, the school sat prominently on a flat stretch of hard, lateritic soil with few trees. In spite of my "training", I was really doubtful that a productive site for the well could be identified. He arrived by bike was quickly ready to get started.

Delays continued as he realized he had forgotten to bring his divining rod. This is not something you can easily find laying around a village. He went back to his bike and began to disassemble the fender. He removed and reshaped the wire used to hold the fender on the bike frame. He was ready to go. He could worry about his fender later.

It took about thirty minutes to walk-off the lines he would use to identify the underground source of water for the well that he determined would be fifty feet deep. Soon after, the elders were satisfied with the site selection and work on the well was begun.

Three weeks later, we found water at a depth of forty-five feet.

No one was surprised but me.

3. *Are You Kidding Me?*

There are some days when working in a well was a fabulous experience. After my first few wells, things become much less complicated. I went to inspect a well that had been dug and deepened by the previous Volunteer. It was not very deep –

maybe twenty feet. It was a shallow well because it was located very near a seasonal streambed that, though often dry for six months of the year, provides a shallow water table.

When a well is first dug, you attempt to go as deep into the water table as possible. As new wells are used, the surrounding water table that had been previously unavailable is now accessible. This accessibility can cause the surrounding water table to drop to a new, lower level. By going deeper into the table with the main well, you can sometimes avoid the need for deepening.

When deepening is needed, you begin to sink smaller diameter concrete sections into the deepened hole below the first well casing of the original well. There are a lot of variables that can affect the outcome of a well. The soil can be hardened clay or soft sand. Digging into a sandier base will be easier to dig but will result in more frequent wall collapse.

If any of the prior concrete sections of the original well are not properly secured to each higher section or if the soil is too soft, the well casings can shift and separate – leaving a gaping hole between it and the lower ground. That is what happened to this well.

I was first in to assess the damage. It would not be difficult to repair the three-foot gap. As I was looking around, I noticed something in the gap of the well. It was alive and moving. I did not hesitate to request being pulled quickly from the well. Since I could not explain what I saw, one of the workers was lowered in to take a look. I saw him reaching into the hole trying to grab whatever was there.

A few minutes later, he was pulled from the well. In one hand, he had a tight grip on the neck of what appeared to be a feral cat. It let everyone know it was not happy. Everyone started laughing that I was afraid of the cat. At the time, it did not seem silly to me. The ingrained paranoia of contracting an incurable infection or rabies remained vivid in my mind.

About a half hour later after working in the safely secured well, someone from above asked if I wanted to come up for something to eat. We had been working for several hours. When I reached the top, I noticed there was fire and something was cooking. It was lunchtime and they asked me which part of the cat I would like to have first.

The prospect of having cat for lunch was not a fabulous experience.

Pig la a ye
11

Closure

"Because we don't think about future generations, they will never forget us."

Henrik Tikkanen

Closure came abruptly but I would not say it came quickly. Those two years spent in the Peace Corps were long and trying. I suffered many infections but fortunately no disease that required evacuation. The well-digging program has been very successful for the Peace Corps. One reason for this success is that wells provide immediate, tangible and beneficial results. Everyone understands the value of a well and the fresh, clean water it can provide.

But the entire Peace Corps experience is more than just delivering needed relief services to remote corners of developing countries. It is a cultural exchange opportunity. I have always felt that the benefits of this exchange were skewed more to me than to the villages I served. Other Volunteers may have had a different opinion.

Some Volunteers walk away culturally richer, others pursue Foreign Service careers. Some leave the program early. The only pressure put upon a Volunteer to stay or leave was the self-directed pressure of the Volunteer.

Environment

Dablo proved to be a good place for me to begin my discovery. Unfortunately, upon return to the States I never took advantage of the power of that experience until many years later. I never considered that those memories might just be the bridge to something much larger in my future.

The quality of our modern environment correlates very closely to the rise and movement of our ancestors and to our daily actions today. Our evolutionary trail is quite well defined. In those ancient early days, life expectancies were low. Ironically, many developing countries are still impacted by similar low, life expectancy levels. Some things our ancestors had control over. Many things they did not. When something like a drought or a severe weather phenomenon occurred, a family could simply pick-up what remained and move to a new and potentially safer location – much like the freedom of today's pastoralist. The environment was perhaps the earliest driver of migration.

Like the pastoralists moving herds throughout the global drylands, they owned little and traveled with less. Herds remained on the move in constant search of better pasture. Those small channels through grasslands and forests eventually became roads. Settlements eventually became cities.

No one knew anything about pollution but that didn't matter since the available space around the planet assured that it would take hundreds of thousands of years for groups to begin having contact with each other. Rivers were pure and flowed freely to flush out unwanted sediments. Fish and animal populations were so numerous that the only reason to not eat would be the incompetency of the individual.

Better yet, there were no lingering debates about climate change and environmental stewardship. The terms had not been invented.

1. More Than A Title

It has been called The Great War, probably because it involved all of the world's major powers. Then, there was the Great Depression – an economic slump that crossed borders from North America and Europe to industrialized areas of the world. Somehow, being tagged "great" adds a special significance.

We forget that there have been a lot of not-so-greats. The Civil War must have been one of the not-so-greats because it was not called the Great Civil War. What if something just has a date – like the 1902 Recession or the Earthquake of 1906? Are those also not-so-greats?

Australia just experienced a drought that lasted twelve years. That certainly could qualify to be called great. This would make the severe drought in Texas that only lasted one year, a not-so-great. There might even be an opportunity to label our present state of environmental issues as the Period of Great Environmental Decline.

Once you get the hang of it, labeling becomes quite easy.

In the future, only historians will be able to tell us if the economic and environmental problems we are experiencing today (their past) should be classified as "great" or "not-so-great".

2. *Common Roots*

To understand our origins, it is sometimes just a simple knowledge of geography and history.

Before we became distinctly separate continents we were one.

About one billion to 500 million years ago – who's really counting, Gondwana collided with North America, Europe, and Siberia to form the supercontinent of Pangea.

The breakup of Gondwana occurred in stages. Some 180 million years ago, the western half of Gondwana (Africa and South America) separated from the eastern half (Madagascar, India, Australia, and Antarctica). The South

Atlantic Ocean opened about 140 million years ago as Africa separated from South America. At about the same time, India, which was still attached to Madagascar, separated from Antarctica and Australia, opening the central Indian Ocean.

As a global community of seven billion neighbors, we often don't appreciate our common ancestral roots.

3. I Could Have Been A Chief

After nearly two years living in my village, the strangeness had long ago disappeared and what had begun as a discovery of culture and self became a time for decision. I had exhausted an attempt to have a well program begun in a drier northern district and made the decision to return home.

Over the final few months, I had the opportunity to say goodbye to many of the people who had shared in my discovery. I guess I had also shared in their discovery.

I had nurtured a special relationship with the resident Fulbe chief – a relationship that remained culturally distant but respectfully close. When he was in the area, he would often come by for a short visit. We both would struggle with Mòoré. Like most Fulbe, he was tall and lean with a light, copper-colored skin tone. These features were distinctively different from the Mossi whose faces were often scarred with tribal markings known as cicatrices and their two front teeth fractured to form a fashionable v-shaped opening.

On one visit, he shared an oral hygiene secret. Fulbe generally have clean, brilliantly white teeth. I never understood how. On this visit, he was using a stick to scrape his teeth. I asked about the stick and he showed me a pre-packaged set of twelve sticks that can be bought in most markets – especially markets frequented by Fulbe. He gave me one to try. Each was roughly square in shape and about four inches in length. The results were fantastic though I always remained concerned about scraping off too much enamel with the plaque.

When he learned that I was planning to leave, he came to visit. Although he had limited knowledge of French and I had little fluency in Fula – the native language of the Fulbe, he was somehow able to make me a final offer.

Would I consider staying?

He would be willing to give me ten head of cattle and I could find several wives. The Fula are Muslim and allowed to have as many as four wives if they can be supported.

I did not accept his offer and we quietly departed each other's company but never friendship. To this day I often wonder if I really could have been chief.

4. *Sounds of the Desert*

My arrival in Agadez was of short-duration – lasting maybe four hours. I was leaving West Africa after two years and was being given a ride to Belgium in a C130 cargo plane operated by the Belgian Air Force. They had been part of a multi-national coalition providing humanitarian aid throughout the Sahel. With their work completed, they would be returning to Europe. The charge d'affaires of the US Embassy introduced me to the captain of the group.

I needed a ride and they had plenty of space. The captain did not even hesitate in saying yes. Three weeks after the chance encounter, I was flying north to Belgium. This was July and I was about to say goodbye to the high temperatures and dry heat of West Africa that had persisted for the previous two years. To make the transition even more uncomfortable, I spent the entire 2,800 mile trip in the cargo area of the plane. There were no acoustics and very low temperatures.

We would have only one stop to make and that was in Agadez, Niger. The airfield was about a fifteen minute walk to town. When I exited the plane, there were two immediate shocks. The first was the sheer heat of the Sahara Desert. The second was the near perfect acoustics of the desert. This must be a regular stopping point for cargo aircraft because there were over fifteen that had landed. Even with the engines still running, there was no noticeable sound.

One final shock was that in this intense, dry heat of the desert, your body shows no visible sign of perspiration. Your skin will have a thick salty residue from the rapidly evaporating perspiration that dries on contact with the hot air.

When I departed the plane in Brussels, it was windy and rainy. The temperature was in the 50s. The signs of home were rapidly beginning to reappear and my body and mind recognized that culture change was about to happen for a second time.

Epilogue

"I'm frequently appalled by the low regard you Earthmen have for life."

Spock, First Officer, Starship Enterprise
"The Galileo Seven"

Scientific programs such as the Hubble Telescope, the Chandra X-Ray Observatory and the International Space Station are just a few of the many programs that have enhanced our knowledge of our planet and our universe. Using programs such as these to continuously improve our knowledge of other regions far beyond our solar system is important. One spectacular photograph taken by the Space Station in 2001, captured the delicate boundary between our planet and space. It was a simple thin blue line of atmosphere. It is difficult to imagine that there is such a fine boundary between the vacuum of space and the atmosphere that gives life to our planet.

However, we cannot neglect the vast amount of data we have been accumulating on the health of planet Earth.

Today, we are seeing a tired and challenged planet. With a constantly growing population in excess of seven billion, natural resources are being taken at alarming rates. Sustainability of this pattern is coming under intense scrutiny. Current consumption patterns can neither ensure sustainability nor availability for future generations. The best reserves of clean water can be found only in dark hidden karsts and aquifers and always remain at risk because of inflowing contamination from polluted surface water sources.

When I arrived in Africa, I expected to see things that I could not imagine. It did not take long for these experiences to exceed my expectations. At that time, I was naive about climate change and endangered species. So how could I know then that the local cab driver in some remote African country could have an intuitive sense that the changes in his local weather patterns might have a global connection?

When I arrived in Africa, I did <u>not</u> expect that the environmental conditions I would be experiencing would be signs of things to come in Australia, India, South America, the American Southwest, the oceans, atmosphere and freshwater systems. I never really considered the human link to all of these conditions that, in our modern world, have become part of something much larger.

The international community is challenged in dealing with rapidly changing global issues. In addition to the need for increased levels of aid to traditional aid recipients, the myriad aid organizations such as the United Nations, CARE,

Doctors Without Borders and OXFAM must meet new challenges to administer aid to increasingly more hostile regions of the world.

At the same time, there is a growing urgency for regulatory compliance to more strict environmental standards. Words are no longer sufficient. Some scientists believe that we have already crossed the threshold where correcting our environment decline is no longer more than just a possibility. Unless actions are taken today to mitigate the damage from our negligence, global conditions will continue to deteriorate at an even more alarming rate and our ability to sustain levels of current production and consumption will be severely challenged, as will providing the increasing levels of humanitarian aid required to address growing global needs.

The past cannot be relived. It can only remain a memory. Memories cannot create change. The future does not yet exist. The present is all that we have. It is our actions taken today that will have the greatest impact of what lies ahead in our future.

Glossary

Environmental Terms / Issues

"Peace, non-violence, human rights and the environment – if only everybody saw these as the seamless whole that they are."

Jonathon Porritt (2012)

Adaptation	When dealing with climate disruption, this is an issue about how to balance the likely need from the disruption and the compassionate impulse to provide financial and other relief to victims of climate disruption.	
Aerosols	Can be broadly classified as one of several types of pollutants that have exceptional "transboundary movement" capabilities.	Pollutants in this group include fires, dust storms and carbon monoxide.

Anthropogenic Factors	Attributable to human activities and/or intervention.	
Aquifer	Water-bearing porous soil or rock strata that yield significant amounts of water to wells.	Aquifer formation must be porous (e.g., sand and gravel or cracks and fractures in more solid rock). Water must be able to flow through and out of the formation in quantities large enough to be significant.
Climate	Long-term statistical distribution of weather patterns. It may be a change in the average weather conditions or a change in the distribution of weather events with respect to an average, for example, greater or fewer extreme weather events.	Climate projections provide abundant evidence that freshwater resources are vulnerable and have the potential to be strongly impacted by climate change, with wide-ranging consequences for human societies and ecosystems.
Climate Change	Long-term change in the statistical distribution of weather patterns over periods of time that range from decades to millions of years.	Climatologists predict significant shifts in global precipitation, with some regions getting wetter and others drier – shifts that will lead to persistent drought and water scarcity in many areas of Africa, the Mediterranean, the Middle East, Central Asia, the Indian

		subcontinent, southern and eastern Australia, northern Mexico, and the southwestern United States.
Desertification	Land degradation in arid, semi-arid, and dry, sub-humid areas resulting from various factors, including climatic variations and human activities.	The causes of desertification are: change in frequency and amount of rainfall, reduction in vegetal cover, wrong agricultural management practices, cultivation on marginal lands, over-exploitation of the natural resources, excessive grazing, etc.
Drought	It is difficult to define drought with a universal definition because it is a relative concept. It varies with location and economic, social, and political context.

The most basic and universally accepted definitions compare supply to need. It is a deficiency in precipitation that leads to deficits in water supply relative to human and environmental needs.

Drought has a physical component (deficiency in precipitation) and an environmental, social, or economic component (need or demand). | Drought can be broadly assigned into four categories.

Meteorological drought: a sustained reduction in precipitation over a defined period of time relative to a defined baseline condition.

Agricultural drought: a deficiency in soil moisture relative to crop or forage needs, leading to reduced crop yield or quality or total crop failures.

Hydrological drought: a deficiency in water |

		storage and flow in natural or artificial systems, including reduced soil moisture, groundwater depth, stream flow, runoff volume, and water levels in lakes and reservoirs. Socioeconomic drought: a deficiency in water relative to some economic need or resource, such as livestock watering, irrigation, hydroelectric power generation, or municipal and industrial use.
Drylands	Drylands are ecosystems characterized by a lack of water. They include cultivated lands, scrublands, shrub lands, grasslands, savannas, semi-deserts and true deserts. Approximately 40 percent of the global land area is considered dryland. The most commonly recognized drylands include the African Sahel, Australian Outback, South American Patagonia, and North American Great Plains.	Australia has more dryland than any other country in the world. Other countries with large amounts of dryland include the United States, Russia, China, and Kazakhstan.
El Nino	The atmospheric component of the El Niño–Southern Oscillation (ENSO) is the most significant mode of inter-annual variability of the global	

		climate. ENSO has global impacts on atmospheric circulation, precipitation and temperature	
	Global Warming	A global atmospheric effect caused by the buildup of greenhouse gases (GHGs) in the atmosphere.	Agriculture today accounts for 14% of total greenhouse gas emissions, with another 17% attributed to land use change linked to deforestation.
	Greenhouse Gasses	Hydrochlorofluorocarbons (HCFCs), currently the most widely used ozone-depleting substance. CO_2: Occurs naturally in landfills, coalmines, paddy fields, natural gas systems, and livestock. N_2O: Generated by burning fossil fuels, in the manufacture of fertilizer and by cultivation of soils. Perflourocarbons (PFCs): Human-made chemicals. A by-product of aluminum smelting. Also used as a replacement for CFCs in manufacturing semiconductors. Sulphur Hexaflouride (SF_6): Used largely in heavy industry to insulate high voltage equipment and to assist in the manufacture of cable cooling systems. Ozone (O_3): Naturally	Ozone at ground level and in the lower atmosphere is linked with smog and health problems. In the upper atmosphere, ozone helps to protect the earth from ultra-violet radiation and chemicals which tend to destroy ozone in the upper atmosphere

	occurring. Also created by reactions involving nitrogen oxide gases resulting from motor vehicles and power plants. Nitrogen Triflouride (NF_3): Commonly used in the manufacturing of flat-panel displays.	
Groundwater	Water beneath the land surface that fills the spaces in rock and sediment.	Groundwater is replenished by precipitation. Under natural conditions much of that recharge returns to the atmosphere by evapo-transpiration from plants and trees or discharges to surface waters. Groundwater discharge to surface waters allows streams to flow beyond rain and snowmelt periods and sustains lake levels during dry spells.
Migration	Major influential factors include: lost job opportunities, wages, similarity of language and culture, social networks, housing and human security in the place of origin and destination.	The climate change scenarios presented by the IPCC have generated estimates that from 150 million to 1 billion people will be displaced

			or forced to migrate. There are 191 million migrants now living outside of their countries of origin today, or 3% of the global population.
			Migration decisions are influenced by many factors, making it difficult to isolate one particular factor as the primary cause of a decision to migrate.
			The average migrant is between 15-35 years of age and could be female or male. In the past forty years the share of female migrants has increased to equal the share of men migrating worldwide.
Mitigation	When dealing with climate disruptions, this is the likely need		

	and compassionate impulse to reduce the overall risk of those impacts from the climate disruption	
Sustainability	Improvements in the quality of human life within the carrying capacity of supporting ecosystems.	Sustainability will be achieved only when development displaces growth; when the scale of the human economy is kept with the capacity of the overall ecosystem upon which it depends.
Weather	The way the atmosphere is behaving in the present time	

www.ingramcontent.com/pod-product-compliance
Lightning Source LLC
Chambersburg PA
CBHW070811100426
42742CB00012B/2332